2025
Lunar Wine Tasting Calendar
A BioDynamic Guide

Ralph DeAmicis & Lahni DeAmicis

Cuore Libre Publishing
Napa California

2025 Lunar Wine Tasting Calendar
A BioDynamic Guide
By Ralph De Amicis & Lahni De Amicis

Published by Cuore Libre Publishing
Napa, California
www.SpaceAndTime.com

Copyright 2025 Ralph & Lahni De Amicis
ISBN 979-8-338799-72-7 No part of this book may be reproduced in any form without permission from the publisher.

Cover Photo: Lahni DeAmicis
Illustrations: Ralph De Amicis
Chapters Two and Three previously appeared in the book, Planetary Calendar Astrology, Moving Beyond Observation into Action by the same authors.

Chapters Four and Five previously appeared in the books, Dream Tours of Napa and Sonoma. and A Tour Guide's Napa Valley by Ralph & Lahni De Amicis.

About the Design: This book was designed to be easy to use. The fonts and spacing are larger than average. The writing style uses shorter sentences, paragraphs and chapters. We have put the books's ergonomics over the aesthetics. Wishing you enjoyment and illumination in your quest for knowledge.

Ralph & Lahni De Amicis

Contents

Introduction: How to Use This Calendar 5

The Moon Signs Quick Reference Guide 7

The Lunar 'Wine Tasting' Calendar includes
Forecast Highlights from the Planetary Calendar with a Month at a Glance and a Week at a Glance Dayplanner
January: 11 - February: 19 - March: 27
April: 35 - May: 43 - June: 51
July: 59 - August: 67 - September: 75
October: 83 - November: 91 - December: 99

Wine Tasting with the Stars
Chapter One: Timing Wine Tastings by the Moon 107
Chapter Two: Fine Wine and the Planets 113
Chapter Three: The Signs as Actions 121

Dream Tours
Chapter Four: Ralph's ABC's for Tasting Wine 133
Chapter Five: Our Best Tasting Room Tips 139

About the Authors 143
Catalog of Books & Calendars 144

The Moon Signs

Plant Part......Sign... Element......Behavior

Bold **Fruit**...............Aries ♈..Fire - Quick Fruit on the Nose

Grounded **Root**..Taurus ♉..Earth- Slow Wood on the Palate

Spring **Flower**.........Gemini ♊..Air - Quick Acid on the Nose

Nurturing **Leaf**....Crab ♋......Water - Slow Savory on Palate

Abundant **Fruit**........... Leo ♌..Fire - Easy Fruit on the Nose

Visible **Root**....Virgo ♍..Earth - Gradual Wood on the Palate

Graceful **Flower**......Libra...♎..Air - Easy Floral on the Nose

Cactus **Leaf**..Scorpio ♏..Water - Slow Phenols on the Palate

Exotic **Fruit**.....Sagittarius ♐..Fire - Long Fruit on the Nose

Climbing **Root**...Capricorn ♑.. Earth - Slow Wood on the Palate

Social **Flower**....Aquarius ♒..Air - Bright Esters on the Nose

Healing **Leaf**...Pisces ♓..Water - Slowly Poignant on the Palate

Introduction: How to Use This Calendar

To use the calendar, look up the date, note the Moon Sign and consult the Quick Reference Guide that follows this Intro. Next, use those insights about how the wines and the guests will react that day to improve your enjoyment of the tasting. That's all there is to it! As a shortcut there are notes on the Calendar pages, and when the Moon changes Sign during business hours, we note that. If you feel like it, read the rest of this introduction.

This book explains how to use the Moon's daily Sign to improve your wine and food tasting experiences. It is based on the work of winemakers who use BioDynamics, an organic farming system created after WWI. They use a specialized astrology calendar for timing tasks, including commercial tastings.

We have expanded on that approach because it gives the mistaken impression that some Moons are good for tasting and others are bad. Every Moon Sign can produce a good experience when you understand that its position affects how quickly wines open, how much they aerate, and the kind of experience people will most enjoy that day.

BioDynamics defines the Moon positions as Fruit, Root, Flower and Leaf. Those describe Astrology's four Elements, Fire, Earth, Air and Water. In science those are the four states of matter, Plasma, Solid, Gaseous and Liquid. Some Winemakers prefer Fruit/Fire and Flower/Air Moons for commercial tastings because their energy is moving up, so the wines open quicker. They avoid doing tastings on the Root/Earth and Leaf/Water Moons because their energy is moving down, so the wines open slower.

But each of the twelve Moon Signs produce unique conditions. Yes, the wines aerate faster on Fruit and Flower days, but speed is not the only factor affecting people's enjoyment of a wine tasting. For instance, a Leaf/Pisces Moon often produces dreamy and romantic tastings, good story telling and intimate conversations. While the wines open slowly, they are experienced on the palate in complex and profound ways. When that mood is promoted, it produces great tasting room sales.

The book also includes monthly forecasts from California's coolest and most informative Astrology calendar, started in 1949. We also includ a dayplanner to record your observations about the wines. To add some context there are three 'Astro' chapters, about using Lunar timing, correlating the Planets to the popular wine styles, and exploring the Astrological Signs as actions. Finally, there are two chapters about enhancing the wine tasting experience which is always fun. Enjoy!

You can find more at PlanetaryCalendar.com

The Moon Sign Quick Reference Guide

Abundant Fruit = Fire – Moon Sign is ♈ Aries: The wines open quickly with strong fruit on the nose, but they may lack staying power. This is an impatient Moon so don't make guests wait a long time between wines. This is one of the days when you can use one glass for the entire tasting, because there is a tendency towards a short attention span. Red wines shine on the Aries Moons, especially the mid-range reds like Zinfandel, Barbera and Malbec.

Grounded Root = Earth – Moon Sign is ♉ Taurus: The wines open very slowly, and the experience is on the palate. Lead the guests through the swirling and sipping. Food pairings with savory flavors enhance the wine's earthy flavors. The guests physical comfort is very important. Play pleasant music in the tasting room, no hard rock! Taurus wines tend to be voluptuous with a strong bouquet.

Spring Flower = Air – Moon Sign is ♊ Gemini: The wines open quickly emphasizing the floral notes and the alcohol. It shows off white wines well although high alcohol red wines need to handled carefully with large glasses. Playful conversation and flirting thrive during this Moon. Be very aware of any odd scents or distractions in the tasting room, and like Aries, don't make guests wait a long time between wines. Pinot Grigio is an example of a Gemini wine.

Nurturing Leaf = Water – Moon Sign is ♋ Cancer: The wines open slowly and benefit from more swirling and water water alongside the wine. Creating an emotionally comfortable and accepting experience is the key. Food pairings should include some cheese. Stories related to the winemaking family will help them connect. Highly tannic wines suffer while sweeter wines like Moscato shine.

Abundant Fruit = Fire – Moon Sign is ♌ Leo: flavors are emphasized, and flavors tend to be well rounded. A more dramatic presentation works well, along with storytelling. The food pairing should be fun and not interfere with the flavors. This is a romantic, dramatic, heart-centered Moon and Chardonnay is a Sun centered, golden Leo wine, so if you have it, start with that and let it shine.

Visible Root = Earth – Moon Sign is ♍ Virgo: The wines open slowly, the food pairing should be refined. This is a Moon for education and sharing the stories of the people behind the vineyards and wines. Virgo Moons are perfectionistic, but they thrive on good conversation. Pinot Noir is a Virgo wine, preferred by a refined palate, especially women, and is considered one of the healthiest wines, because of its high nutrients and restrained tannins and alcohol.

Graceful Flower = Air – Moon Sign is ♎ Libra: The wines open quickly emphasizing the floral notes and the alcohol. It shows off white wines well although high alcohol red wines need to managed carefully with large glasses. Libra is a Venus Ruled Sign, and this is a favorite Sign for couples, so highlighting the wines that they both will like is a winner. Any food pairing should be elegant and pleasing to the eye. Sauvignon Blanc is a Libra wine, balanced and elegant rather than passionate, and it ages well.

Cactus Leaf = Water – Moon Sign is ♏ Scorpio: The wines open slowly and give up their flavors gradually, but they connect on a passionate level. Guests are often very guarded with their comments during this Moon, so it's important to lead them through extensive swirling, and have them come back the to wines after they've had a chance to open more. Petite Verdot is a Scorpio wine, dark, deep with a transformative power. On Water Moons guests emotions are being triggered by the flavors during the experience. Any food pairing should be capped with dark chocolate.

Exotic Fruit = Fire – Moon Sign is ♐ Sagittarius: The wines open quickly emphasizing the fruit, and the flavors have more staying power, so it favors tastings with multiple glasses. Discussions tend to be lively and there is often one upmanship that happens with guests showing off one's wine knowledge and familiarity with diverse regions, in a fun way. Emphasize the prospects of the wine and offer pairings that are bit exotic and playful. A big, flavorful Merlot is a Sagittarius wine.

Climbing Root = Earth – Moon Sign is ♑ Capricorn: This is the most structured of the Earth Signs and like the others the wines open slowly and benefit from a savory pairing. Sauvignon Cabernet is a Capricorn wine, tannic, age worthy and serious. People tend to be emotionally reserved on Capricorn Moons and the prestige of the wine matters. Adding a touch of formality and letting the wines continue to open will make a big difference. Like the other Earth Signs a food pairing will help pace the tasting to the wine's best advantage. Like Scorpio, any pairing should be capped with dark chocolate.

Social Flower = Air – Moon Sign is ♒ Aquarius: The wines open quickly and tend to bring the florals notes forward, although in a high alcohol wine, the fumes need extra time and swirling to move out of the way. This is a Moon that loves anything unusual in your line of wines, the innovative and exotic will be happily explored. Any food pairing should come with an explanation and discussion about why it was chosen for the wines. This is very much like a Gemini Moon, thriving on conversation, maybe with less levity, but more brilliance. This is a very visual Moon so point out the colors of the wine to engage your guests.

Healing Leaf = Water – Moon Sign is ♓ Pisces: Water Moons tend to be emotionally complex, sometimes that works in your favor. The Pisces Moon is about dreaminess and imagination which resonate wonderfully with the good feelings and intoxication implicit in a wine tasting. It is during March in the Pisces time of year in California, that new buds appear on the vines, so tastings tend towards an only slightly restrained joyfulness. Make sure the clients stay hydrated and don't overdo the food pairing, although adding a touch of something salty is appropriate because Pisces, the Dolphins, are associated with the ocean.

January Forecasts
Highlights from the Planetary Calendar
Capricorn the Sea Goat to Aquarius the Water Pourer

The year starts with Mars, Jupiter and Uranus Retrograde, but a fast Mercury, so at least communications will run smoothly. That Mars in Cancer may cause physical frustrations and by the Full Moon on the 13th that may boil over a bit, so be careful. Jupiter Retrograde in Gemini Square Saturn in Pisces, Conjunct Venus, may cause challenges for the economy. Expect people to be talking about their worries, so give that a pass if you want to avoid the static.

13th - The Full Moon on the 13th is complex with Aspects to Mars, Uranus and Neptune, so issues of national or global significance will intrude on people's consciousness.

19th - The Sun enters Aquarius with a Libra Moon Trine Jupiter in Gemini and Mercury Sextile Venus, so this is a wonderful day for socializing and good conversations. With the Sun joining Pluto there may be a sense of hidden power at this time.

29th - The New Moon at 9 degrees Aquarius picks up some energy from Jupiter in Gemini, all the Air Signs will feel charged up. Seven of the ten bodies are in either Aquarius or Pisces so there will be a sense at the New Moon that events are wrapping up. See our annual Lunar New Year Forecast online at PlanetaryCalendar.com.

2025 Lunar Tasting Calendar

Bold Fruit: Wines open quickly, fruit forward, guests enthusiastically share opinions. **Grounded Root:** Wine open slowly but deliciously, don't rush and play pleasant music. **Spring Flowers:** Wines open quickly, acid forward, guests like to flirt and play.

JANUARY 2025

SUNDAY	MONDAY	TUESDAY
Bold Fruit **5** Aries Moon	Bold Fruit **6** Aries Moon	Grounded Root **7** Taurus Moon Beginning 2:11pm
Nurturing Leaf **12** Cancer Moon	Full Moon Nurturing Leaf **13** Cancer Moon	Abundant Fruit **14** Leo Moon
Graceful Flower **19** Libra Moon	Graceful Flower **20** Libra Moon	Cactus Leaf **21** Scorpio Moon
Climbing Root **26** Capricorn Moon	Climbing Root **27** Capricorn Moon	Social Flower **28** Aquarius Moon

Graceful Flowers: Wines open gracefully, florals forward, guests slow to decide, patience. **Cactus Leaf:** Wines open gradually but deeply, guests will experience the wines emotionally. **Exotic Fruit:** Wines open enthusiastically, expect conversations to range far and wide.

Nurturing Leaf: Wines open slowly & voluptuously, help guests feel at home. **Abundant Fruit:** Wines open easily and generously, guests like to share their feelings about the wine. **Visible Roots:** Wines open carefully and thoughtfully, guests will want more info and details.

Wednesday	Thursday	Friday	Saturday
Social Flower **1** Aquarius Moon	Social Flower **2** Aquarius Moon	Healing Leaf **3** Pisces Moon	Healing Leaf **4** Pisces Moon
Grounded Root **8** Taurus Moon	Grounded Root **9** Taurus Moon	Spring Flower **10** Gemini Moon	Spring Flower **11** Gemini Moon
Abundant Fruit **15** Leo Moon	Visible Roots **16** Virgo Moon	Visible Roots **17** Virgo Moon	Visible Roots **18** Virgo Moon
Cactus Leaf **22** Scorpio Moon	Cactus Leaf **23** Scorpio Moon	Exotic Fruit **24** Sagittarius Moon	Exotic Fruit **25** Sagittarius Moon
Social Flower **29** Aquarius Moon	New Moon Healing Leaf **30** Pisces Moon	Lunar New Year Social Flower **31** Aquarius Moon Beginning 2:52pm	

Calculated for Pacific Clock Time

Climbing Root: Wines open slowly tannins forward, comments come when alcohol hits. **Social Flower:** Wines open broadly, esters forward, conversations take unexpected turns. **Healing Leaf:** Wines open patiently and dreamily, story telling and imagination soars.

2025 Lunar Tasting Calendar

December 31 through 5

MONDAY 30	
TUESDAY 31	
WEDNESDAY 1	
THURSDAY 2	
FRIDAY 3	
SATURDAY 4	
SUNDAY 5	

January 6 through 12

	MONDAY 6
	TUESDAY 7
	WEDNESDAY 8
	THURSDAY 9
	FRIDAY 10
	SATURDAY 11
	SUNDAY 12

January 13 through 19

MONDAY 13	
TUESDAY 14	
WEDNESDAY 15	
THURSDAY 16	
FRIDAY 17	
SATURDAY 18	
SUNDAY 19	

January 20 through 26

	MONDAY 20
	TUESDAY 21
	WEDNESDAY 22
	THURSDAY 23
	FRIDAY 24
	SATURDAY 25
	SUNDAY 26

18 2025 Lunar Tasting Calendar

January 27 through 31

MONDAY 27	
TUESDAY 28	
WEDNESDAY 29	
THURSDAY 30	
FRIDAY 31	

February Forecasts
Highlights from the Planetary Calendar
Aquarius the Water Pourer to Pisces the Fishes

Some of the congestion and frustration of January fades as February progresses. After the 23rd, all the Planets are direct so events and projects will move forward more easily. Only Mercury and Venus change Signs so there isn't too much turbulence. Plus, they both move into Signs that work well in the home life, so this is a good time to improve your close relationships. With four White Circle Days and two Black Box days it's an easy month. Watch out, in the later part of the month Mercury is slowing, preparing to turn Retrograde on March 14th, so those kinds of communication projects will not move forward as easily.

12th - The Full Moon at 24 degrees Leo and Aquarius is Square Uranus so there may be disruptions to the electrical grid, or some type of extreme weather or geological event. If you have planets Square this opposition, at 24 degrees Fixed, Taurus and Scorpio, you may feel challenged, but take the opportunity to accomplish tasks despite the obstructions.

18th - The Sun enters Pisces while the Scorpio Moon makes a Trine to Mercury in Pisces, a wonderfully comfortable day for the Water Signs. **27th -** The New Moon finds five Planets and Ceres in Pisces in a loose Square to Jupiter in Gemini and a Trine to Mars in Scorpio. All of this activity can be distracting so remember that the solution to distraction is action.

Bold Fruit: Wines open quickly, fruit forward, guests enthusiastically share opinions. **Grounded Root:** Wine open slowly but deliciously, don't rush and play pleasant music. **Spring Flowers:** Wines open quickly, acid forward, guests like to flirt and play games.

FEBRUARY 2025

SUNDAY	MONDAY	TUESDAY
Bold Fruit **2** Aries Moon	Bold Fruit **3** Aries Moon	Grounded Root **4** Taurus Moon
Nurturing Leaf **9** Cancer Moon	Abundant Fruit **10** Leo Moon	Abundant Fruit **11** Leo Moon
Graceful Flower **16** Libra Moon	Cactus Leaf **17** Scorpio Moon Beginning 4:18pm	Cactus Leaf **18** Scorpio Moon
Climbing Root **23** Capricorn Moon	Climbing Root **24** Capricorn Moon	Social Flower **25** Aquarius Moon

Graceful Flowers: Wines open gracefully, florals forward, guests slow to decide, patience. **Cactus Leaf:** Wines open gradually but deeply, guests will experience the wines emotionally. **Exotic Fruit:** Wines open enthusiastically, expect conversations to range far and wide.

Nurturing Leaf: Wines open slowly & voluptuously, help guests feel at home. **Abundant Fruit:** Wines open easily and generously, guests like to share their feelings about the wine. **Visible Roots:** Wines open carefully and thoughtfully, guests will want more info and details.

WEDNESDAY	THURSDAY	FRIDAY	SATURDAY
			Healing Leaf **1** Pisces Moon
Grounded Root **5** Taurus Moon	Spring Flower **6** Gemini Moon	Spring Flower **7** Gemini Moon	Nurturing Leaf **8** Cancer Moon
Full Moon Abundant Fruit **12** Leo Moon	Visible Roots **13** Virgo Moon	Visible Roots **14** Virgo Moon	Graceful Flower **15** Libra Moon
Cactus Leaf **19** Scorpio Moon	Exotic Fruit **20** Sagittarius Moon	Exotic Fruit **21** Sagittarius Moon	Climbing Root **22** Capricorn Moon Beginning 3:08pm
Social Flower **26** Aquarius Moon	New Moon Healing Leaf **27** Pisces Moon	Healing Leaf **28** Pisces Moon	

Calculated for Pacific Clock Time

Climbing Root: Wines open slowly tannins forward, comments come when alcohol hits. **Social Flower:** Wines open broadly, esters forward, conversations take unexpected turns. **Healing Leaf:** Wines open patiently and dreamily, story telling and imagination soars.

February 1 through 2

SATURDAY 1	
SUNDAY 2	

February 3 through 9

	MONDAY 3
	TUESDAY 4
	WEDNESDAY 5
	THURSDAY 6
	FRIDAY 7
	SATURDAY 8
	SUNDAY 9

February 10 through 16

MONDAY 10	
TUESDAY 11	
WEDNESDAY 12	
THURSDAY 13	
FRIDAY 14	
SATURDAY 15	
SUNDAY 16	

February 17 through 23

	MONDAY 17
	TUESDAY 18
	WEDNESDAY 19
	THURSDAY 20
	FRIDAY 21
	SATURDAY 22
	SUNDAY 23

February 24 through 28

MONDAY 24	
TUESDAY 25	
WEDNESDAY 26	
THURSDAY 27	
FRIDAY 28	

March Forecasts
Highlights from the Planetary Calendar
Pisces the Fishes to Aries the Ram

As mild and astrologically uneventful February was, March wants all the attention and it is filled with events. *There is a Total Lunar Eclipse on the 13th followed by a Partial Solar Eclipse on the 29th* so those two weeks in between will be emotionally complex and potentially difficult depending on where they fall in your chart.

Neptune enters Aries on the 30th which by itself is a big event. This Planet is associated with the gases and chemicals that our modern technological world depends on, so when it moves into the Martial Sign of new beginnings it can signal explosive innovation. As Neptune moves through Aries over the next fourteen years, expect to see a greater awareness of how household and industrial chemicals affect our bodies, and an increased move towards personalized pharmaceuticals.

Also, *Mercury and Venus both turn Retrograde* so personal issues and communication may become a little frustrating if this impacts your personal Planets. The days near the Eclipses are packed with complex Aspects. The forecast continuess on page 30.

Bold Fruit: Wines open quickly, fruit forward, guests enthusiastically share opinions. **Grounded Root:** Wine open slowly but deliciously, don't rush and play pleasant music. **Spring Flowers:** Wines open quickly, acid forward, guests like to flirt and play games.

MARCH 2025

SUNDAY	MONDAY	TUESDAY
Grounded Root **30** Taurus Moon Beginning 1:15pm	Grounded Root **31** Taurus Moon	
Bold Fruit **2** Aries Moon	Grounded Root **3** Taurus Moon	Grounded Root **4** Taurus Moon
Abundant Fruit **9** Leo Moon Beginning 3:58pm	Abundant Fruit **10** Leo Moon	Abundant Fruit **11** Leo Moon
Graceful Flower **16** Libra Moon	Cactus Leaf **17** Scorpio Moon	Cactus Leaf **18** Scorpio Moon
Climbing Root **23** Capricorn Moon	Full Moon Eclipse Social Flower **24** Aquarius Moon	Social Flower **25** Aquarius Moon

Graceful Flowers: Wines open gracefully, florals forward, guests slow to decide, patience. **Cactus Leaf:** Wines open gradually but deeply, guests will experience the wines emotionally. **Exotic Fruit:** Wines open enthusiastically, expect conversations to range far and wide.

March 29

Nurturing Leaf: Wines open slowly & voluptuously, help guests feel at home. **Abundant Fruit:** Wines open easily and generously, guests like to share their feelings about the wine. **Visible Roots:** Wines open carefully and thoughtfully, guests will want more info and details.

WEDNESDAY	THURSDAY	FRIDAY	SATURDAY
			Bold Fruit **1** Aries Moon
Spring Flower **5** Gemini Moon	Spring Flower **6** Gemini Moon	Nurturing Leaf **7** Cancer Moon	Nurturing Leaf **8** Cancer Moon
Visible Roots **12** Virgo Moon	Full Moon Eclipse Visible Roots **13** Virgo Moon	Graceful Flower **14** Libra Moon Beginning 11:58am	Graceful Flower **15** Libra Moon
Exotic Fruit **19** Sagittarius Moon Beginning 1:16pm	Exotic Fruit **20** Sagittarius Moon	Exotic Fruit **21** Sagittarius Moon	Climbing Root **22** Capricorn Moon
Healing Leaf **26** Pisces Moon Beginning 12:31pm	Healing Leaf **27** Pisces Moon	Bold Fruit **28** Aries Moon Beginning 1:35pm	New Moon Eclipse Bold Fruit **29** Aries Moon

Calculated for Pacific Clock Time

Climbing Root: Wines open slowly tannins forward, comments come when alcohol hits. **Social Flower:** Wines open broadly, esters forward, conversations take unexpected turns. **Healing Leaf:** Wines open patiently and dreamily, story telling and imagination soars.

March 1 through 2nd

13th - The Total Lunar Eclipse at 23 degrees Virgo and Pisces places Saturn Conjunct the Sun, in the Sign when the old season fades into the new Spring. Be careful with your thoughts and focus on being optimistic because there will be people who may be losing hope or wearing down with worry. Get together with the people you care about and herd them towards the future. That Mars in Cancer Trine the Sun, and Sextile the Moon, shows that a good walk, cooking and enjoyable household projects will make all the difference in our mood. For the next two weeks, people will feel emotionally bound up so be gentle and kind.

20th - Welcome to Spring! The first day of Aries sees the Sun entering the Sign near Venus. While there will be some lingering worries, thanks to the Moon in Sagittarius and Jupiter in Gemini, there will be a youthful optimism welling up. Aries, begin counting down to your Solar Return!

29th - The Partial Solar Eclipse at 9 degrees Aries coincides with Mercury backing into Pisces, and Neptune entering Aries the next day, so hold onto your smart phone. With Mars and Saturn in feminine (responsive) Signs, we see the growing power of women in significant roles of responsibility.

SATURDAY 1	
SUNDAY 2	

March 3 through 9

	MONDAY 3
	TUESDAY 4
	WEDNESDAY 5
	THURSDAY 6
	FRIDAY 7
	SATURDAY 8
	SUNDAY 9

March 10 through 16

MONDAY 10	
TUESDAY 11	
WEDNESDAY 12	
THURSDAY 13	
FRIDAY 14	
SATURDAY 15	
SUNDAY 16	

March 17 through 23

	MONDAY 17
	TUESDAY 18
	WEDNESDAY 19
	THURSDAY 20
	FRIDAY 21
	SATURDAY 22
	SUNDAY 23

34 2025 Lunar Tasting Calendar

March 24 through 31

MONDAY **24** Graceful Flower	
TUESDAY **25**	
WEDNESDAY **26**	
THURSDAY **27**	
FRIDAY **28**	
SATURDAY **29**	
SUNDAY **30**	**MONDAY** **31**

April Forecasts
Highlights from the Planetary Calendar
Aries the Ram to Taurus the Bull

The first seven days of the month are filled with Aspects including *Mercury turning Direct on the 7th,* so Mercury is moving slowly so those kinds of the communication issues will take extra effort to make them work. Venus turns Direct on the 12th and after that, all the Planets are moving forward so we are entering a time when projects can be moved along easily. *The Full Moon aligns with the Star Spica, the brightest in the Constellation Virgo and a feminine archetype,* so expect women's issues to be highlighted. Before and after the Taurus Ingress there are numerous Aspects so expect those few days to be stressful. By the New Moon on the 27th there may be a sense of teetering on the edge between the past and future. When Venus enters Aries on the 30th there will be a sense of finally moving beyond that. **12th -** This is a powerful Full Moon at 23 degrees Libra. This is a good time to focus on your self-healing and personal surroundings. Venus turns Direct further empowering this day. **19th -** The Sun enters Taurus, leading the other personal Planets. This is when the leaves fill out. On the 20th the Sun will Square Mars in Leo. Look at where zero degrees Taurus and Leo are in your chart because there may be tension between those parts of your life, which can be resolved with productive actions. Forecast continues on page 38.

Bold Fruit: Wines open quickly, fruit forward, guests enthusiastically share opinions. **Grounded Root:** Wine open slowly but deliciously, don't rush and play pleasant music. **Spring Flowers:** Wines open quickly, acid forward, guests like to flirt and play games.

APRIL 2025

Sunday	Monday	Tuesday
		Spring Flower **1** Gemini Moon
Abundant Fruit **6** Leo Moon	Abundant Fruit **7** Leo Moon	Visible Roots **8** Virgo Moon
Cactus Leaf **13** Scorpio Moon	Cactus Leaf **14** Scorpio Moon	Cactus Leaf **15** Scorpio Moon
Social Flower **20** Aquarius Moon Beginning 4:21 pm	Social Flower **21** Aquarius Moon	Social Flower **22** Aquarius Moon
New Moon Grounded Root **27** Taurus Moon	Grounded Root **28** Taurus Moon	Spring Flower **29** Gemini Moon

Graceful Flowers: Wines open gracefully, florals forward, guests slow to decide, patience. **Cactus Leaf:** Wines open gradually but deeply, guests will experience the wines emotionally. **Exotic Fruit:** Wines open enthusiastically, expect conversations to range far and wide.

April 37

Nurturing Leaf: Wines open slowly & voluptuously, help guests feel at home. **Abundant Fruit:** Wines open easily and generously, guests like to share their feelings about the wine. **Visible Roots:** Wines open carefully and thoughtfully, guests will want more info and details.

WEDNESDAY	THURSDAY	FRIDAY	SATURDAY
Spring Flower **2** Gemini Moon	Nurturing Leaf **3** Cancer Moon Beginning 3:39 pm	Nurturing Leaf **4** Cancer Moon	Nurturing Leaf **5** Cancer Moon
Visible Roots **9** Virgo Moon	Visible Roots **10** Virgo Moon	Graceful Flower **11** Libra Moon	Full Moon Graceful Flower **12** Libra Moon
Exotic Fruit **16** Sagittarius Moon	Exotic Fruit **17** Sagittarius Moon	Climbing Root **18** Capricorn Moon	Climbing Root **19** Capricorn Moon
Healing Leaf **23** Pisces Moon	Healing Leaf **24** Pisces Moon	Bold Fruit **25** Aries Moon	Bold Fruit **26** Aries Moon
Spring Flower **30** Gemini Moon			

Calculated for Pacific Clock Time

Climbing Root: Wines open slowly tannins forward, comments come when alcohol hits. **Social Flower:** Wines open broadly, esters forward, conversations take unexpected turns. **Healing Leaf:** Wines open patiently and dreamily, story telling and imagination soars.

April 1 through 6

	27th - The New Moon at 7 degrees Taurus, while Mars is in early Taurus, may feel like a cow in a China shop. Tempers may clash with stubbornness so stay on your toes.
TUESDAY 1	
WEDNESDAY 2	
THURSDAY 3	
FRIDAY 4	
SATURDAY 5	
SUNDAY 6	

April 7 through 13

	MONDAY 7
	TUESDAY 8
	WEDNESDAY 9
	THURSDAY 10
	FRIDAY 11
	SATURDAY 12
	SUNDAY 13

April 14 through 20

MONDAY 14	
TUESDAY 15	
WEDNESDAY 16	
THURSDAY 17	
FRIDAY 18	
SATURDAY 29	
SUNDAY 20	

April 21 through 27

	MONDAY 21
	TUESDAY 22
	WEDNESDAY 23
	THURSDAY 24
	FRIDAY 25
	SATURDAY 26
	SUNDAY 27

April 28 through 30

MONDAY 28	
TUESDAY 29	
WEDNESDAY 30	

May Forecasts
Highlights from the Planetary Calendar
Taurus the Bull to Gemini the Twins

The big event this month is Saturn entering Aries on the 24th. In this position there is a tendency to challenge authority, and that results in martyrs being created. The Saturn cycle is 28 years so, in pre-modern times, that was seen as not only the marker of maturity, but often the marker of old age. That's why Saturn has been connected to Father Time. Despite the fact that Astrologers in the 1930's made Capricorn its sole Ruled Sign, in reality, it is equally related to Aquarius and leans towards the masculine there. In Aries, Saturn will challenge the old, conservative structures of Capricorn and Cancer, and encourage the technological innovators of Aquarius and Leo. *The other big event is Pluto turning Retrograde in Aquarius on the 4th.* Before this, all the Planets were moving Direct which encourages progress, so this is the first, subtle hint of slowing. But it's not until July that other Planets begin turning Retrograde and the pace slows significantly and rapid progress will be harder to achieve. **12th -** The Full Moon at 22 degrees Scorpio and Taurus happens amid loose aspects with Saturn and Uranus. Meanwhile Mercury is Square Pluto, so there will be some odd tensions around it. People in committed relationships should tip their toe in for a few days to avoid arguments. Forecast continues on page 46.

44   2025 Lunar Tasting Calendar

Bold Fruit: Wines open quickly, fruit forward, guests enthusiastically share opinions. **Grounded Root:** Wine open slowly but deliciously, don't rush and play pleasant music. **Spring Flowers:** Wines open quickly, acid forward, guests like to flirt and play games.

MAY 2025

Sunday	Monday	Tuesday
Abundant Fruit **4** Leo Moon	Abundant Fruit **5** Leo Moon	New Moon Visible Roots **6** Virgo Moon
Cactus Leaf **11** Scorpio Moon	Cactus Leaf **12** Scorpio Moon	Exotic Fruit **13** Sagittarius Moon
Social Flower **18** Aquarius Moon	Social Flower **19** Aquarius Moon	Healing Leaf **20** Pisces Moon
Grounded Root **25** Taurus Moon	Spring Flower **26** Gemini Moon Beginning 10:21am	Spring Flower **27** Gemini Moon

Graceful Flowers: Wines open gracefully, florals forward, guests slow to decide, patience. **Cactus Leaf:** Wines open gradually but deeply, guests will experience the wines emotionally. **Exotic Fruit:** Wines open enthusiastically, expect conversations to range far and wide.

Nurturing Leaf: Wines open slowly & voluptuously, help guests feel at home. **Abundant Fruit:** Wines open easily and generously, guests like to share their feelings about the wine. **Visible Roots:** Wines open carefully and thoughtfully, guests will want more info and details.

WEDNESDAY	THURSDAY	FRIDAY	SATURDAY
	Nurturing Leaf **1** Cancer Moon	Nurturing Leaf **2** Cancer Moon	Abundant Fruit **3** Leo Moon
Visible Roots **7** Virgo Moon	Graceful Flower **8** Libra Moon	Graceful Flower **9** Libra Moon	Cactus Leaf **10** Scorpio Moon Beginning 12:58 pm
Exotic Fruit **14** Sagittarius Moon	Climbing Root **15** Capricorn Moon Beginning 12:57 pm	Climbing Root **16** Capricorn Moon	Climbing Root **17** Capricorn Moon
Healing Leaf **21** Pisces Moon	Full Moon Bold Fruit **22** Aries Moon	Bold Fruit **23** Aries Moon	Grounded Root **24** Taurus Moon Beginning 10:37am
Nurturing Leaf **28** Cancer Moon Beginning 10:32am	Nurturing Leaf **29** Cancer Moon	Abundant Fruit **30** Leo Moon Beginning 1:16pm	Abundant Fruit **31** Leo Moon

Calculated for Pacific Clock Time

Climbing Root: Wines open slowly tannins forward, comments come when alcohol hits. **Social Flower:** Wines open broadly, esters forward, conversations take unexpected turns. **Healing Leaf:** Wines open patiently and dreamily, story telling and imagination soars.

May 1 through 4

20th - The Sun enters Gemini, Square the Moon and Sextile Saturn, so there will be a serious tone to the Sun's Ingress. But hope springs eternal, because the Sun is joining Jupiter in Gemini, so the Air Signs will feel empowered.

26th - This New Moon at 6 degrees of Gemini is concentrated in Air and Fire Signs, so expect lots of activity and potential discord. Although this is a great time for flirting and moving potential relationships along. This should be an especially social Memorial Day.

THURSDAY 1

FRIDAY 2

SATURDAY 3

SUNDAY 4

May 5 through 11

	MONDAY 5
	TUESDAY 6
	WEDNESDAY 7
	THURSDAY 8
	FRIDAY 9
	SATURDAY 10
	SUNDAY 11

May 12 through 18

MONDAY 12	
TUESDAY 13	
WEDNESDAY 14	
THURSDAY 15	
FRIDAY 16	
SATURDAY 17	
SUNDAY 18	

May 19 through 25

	MONDAY 19
	TUESDAY 20
	WEDNESDAY 21
	THURSDAY 22
	FRIDAY 23
	SATURDAY 24
	SUNDAY 25

May 26 through 31

MONDAY 26	
TUESDAY 27	
WEDNESDAY 28 Social Flower	
THURSDAY 29	
FRIDAY 30	
FRIDAY 31	

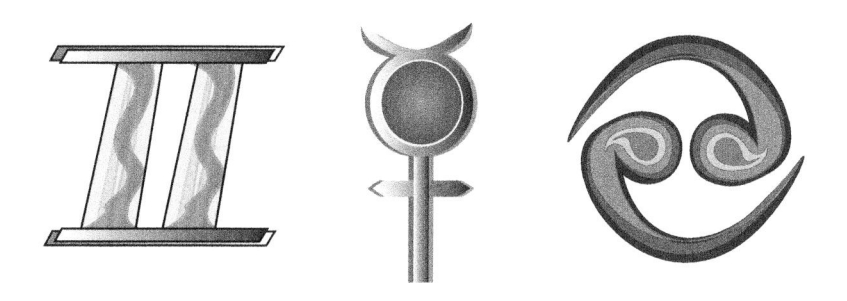

June Forecasts
Highlights from the Planetary Calendar
Gemini the Twins to Cancer the Crab

This is an easier month in many ways than the earlier part of the year with two significant events. Jupiter enters its Exalted Sign of Cancer on the 9th. This means that Jupiter is connected to the Moon, so issues related to women and the home will see the benefits. The fact that Jupiter will be Square Saturn is harder on the economy, but it does show opportunities for improving the ways we can work with our family at home to create personal improvements. *Jupiter will spend the rest of the year in Cancer, turning Retrograde at 25 degrees on November 11th so look for where this is happening in your chart because that area wants to expand.* Heads up Cancer Natives, Jupiter Transits are fun but watch out for overdoing things in terms of food and exercise. *The other big event is the Summer Solstice when the Sun enters Cancer. Historically, the Sun ruled Leo and Cancer, and the Sign of the Crab was the image that described women as leaders.* Why? Because this time year, while the men were hunting, the women would lead the tribe and the children to the cool shorelines to hunt crabs and the roast them on fires made from driftwood. Forecast continues on page 54.

Bold Fruit: Wines open quickly, fruit forward, guests enthusiastically share opinions. **Grounded Root:** Wine open slowly but deliciously, don't rush and play pleasant music. **Spring Flowers:** Wines open quickly, acid forward, guests like to flirt and play games.

JUNE 2025

Sunday	Monday	Tuesday
Abundant Fruit **1** Leo Moon	Visible Roots **2** Virgo Moon	Visible Roots **3** Virgo Moon
Cactus Leaf **8** Scorpio Moon	Exotic Fruit **9** Sagittarius Moon	Exotic Fruit **10** Sagittarius Moon
Social Flower **15** Aquarius Moon	Healing Leaf **16** Pisces Moon Beginning 1:08am	Healing Leaf **17** Pisces Moon
Grounded Root **22** Taurus Moon	Spring Flower **23** Gemini Moon	Spring Flower **24** Gemini Moon
Visible Roots **29** Virgo Moon	Visible Roots **30** Virgo Moon	

Graceful Flowers: Wines open gracefully, florals forward, guests slow to decide, patience. **Cactus Leaf:** Wines open gradually but deeply, guests will experience the wines emotionally. **Exotic Fruit:** Wines open enthusiastically, expect conversations to range far and wide.

Nurturing Leaf: Wines open slowly & voluptuously, help guests feel at home. **Abundant Fruit:** Wines open easily and generously, guests like to share their feelings about the wine. **Visible Roots:** Wines open carefully and thoughtfully, guests will want more info and details.

WEDNESDAY	THURSDAY	FRIDAY	SATURDAY
Graceful Flower **4** Libra Moon	New Moon Graceful Flower **5** Libra Moon	Graceful Flower **6** Libra Moon	Cactus Leaf **7** Scorpio Moon
Full Moon Exotic Fruit **11** Sagittarius Moon	Climbing Root **12** Capricorn Moon	Climbing Root **13** Capricorn Moon	Social Flower **14** Aquarius Moon
Bold Fruit **18** Aries Moon Beginning 4:07pm	Bold Fruit **19** Aries Moon	Bold Fruit **20** Aries Moon	Grounded Root **21** Taurus Moon
New Moon Nurturing Leaf **25** Cancer Moon	Abundant Fruit **26** Leo Moon Beginning 11:05pm	Abundant Fruit **27** Leo Moon	Abundant Fruit **28** Leo Moon

Calculated for Pacific Clock Time

Climbing Root: Wines open slowly tannins forward, comments come when alcohol hits. **Social Flower:** Wines open broadly, esters forward, conversations take unexpected turns. **Healing Leaf:** Wines open patiently and dreamily, story telling and imagination soars.

June 1

9th - A fast moving Jupiter enters its Exalted Sign of Cancer, so look for that in your chart because there are possibilities waiting for you in that part of your life. This is great for the Water Signs, although the Cancerians may find dealing with this much attention challenging.

11th - Even though the Sun is in Gemini, an Air Sign, this chart is all about Earth, Water and Fire, including that Sagittarius Full Moon at 20 degrees being supported by Mars in Leo. Don't be surprised if people are impetuous and it may be difficult to get much accomplished between now and the New Moon.

20th - The Sun enters Cancer at the Summer Solstice, the longest few days of the year. Mercury Square the Moon happens early in the day, but supportive Mars and Jupiter Aspects happen later when the Moon enters Taurus. The highlight is when the Sun joins Jupiter in Cancer. This is one of the best times to travel to someplace cool with people you care about.

25th – Finally, after that very distracted Full Moon, and distracting Void Of Course with the Jupiter Sun Conjunction, this New Moon at 4 degrees Cancer is all about getting things done. So, get your tools in order.

SUNDAY

1

June 2 through 8

	MONDAY 2
	TUESDAY 3
	WEDNESDAY 4
	THURSDAY 5
	FRIDAY 6
	SATURDAY 7
	SUNDAY 8

June 9 through 15

MONDAY 9	
TUESDAY 10	
WEDNESDAY 11	
THURSDAY 12	
FRIDAY 13	
SATURDAY 14	
SUNDAY 15	

June 16 through 22

	MONDAY 16
	TUESDAY 17
	WEDNESDAY 18
	THURSDAY 19
	FRIDAY 20
	SATURDAY 21
	SUNDAY 22

June 23 through 30

MONDAY 23	
TUESDAY 24	
WEDNESDAY 25	
THURSDAY 26	
FRIDAY 27	
SATURDAY 28	
SUNDAY 29	**MONDAY** 30

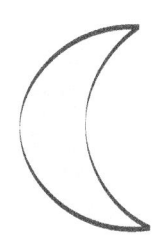

July Forecasts
Highlights from the Planetary Calendar
Cancer the Crab to Leo the Lion

This is another eventful month. Mercury turns Retrograde along with Neptune and Saturn, so the outer worlds of politics and commerce are slowing down. But Venus is moving fast, so your personal life has the wind in its sails. *The big event on the 7th is Uranus leaving Taurus for Gemini. In Taurus,* its disrupting influence has been focused on the climate and money. Its orbit is eighty-four years, so it stays in a Sign on average for about 7 years. The last time Uranus was in Gemini was at the beginning of World War II, and the time before that was just before the American Civil War. The entire conflict took place with Uranus in Gemini. The time before that was during the Revolutionary War, and the USA was founded with Uranus and Mars in Gemini. *This year, it will move forward and then Retrograde back into Taurus on November 7th, then turn Direct and return to Gemini in May of 2026 until May of 2033.* So, now we are getting a taste of how Uranus acts in Gemini. The last time it entered Gemini, the USA had just entered WWII and the battle for democracy was on. The day before Uranus entered Gemini, women became official members of the USA military for the first time. In the middle of the transit, large numbers of refugees were relocating, and the state of Israel was founded. *Uranus is not a Planet that you want to ignore. Go to pg 66.*

Bold Fruit: Wines open quickly, fruit forward, guests enthusiastically share opinions. **Grounded Root:** Wine open slowly but deliciously, don't rush and play pleasant music. **Spring Flowers:** Wines open quickly, acid forward, guests like to flirt and play games.

JULY 2025

Sunday	Monday	Tuesday
		Graceful Flower **1** Libra Moon Beginning 2:16pm
Exotic Fruit **6** Sagittarius Moon Beginning 3:05pm	Exotic Fruit **7** Sagittarius Moon	Exotic Fruit **8** Sagittarius Moon
Healing Leaf **13** Pisces Moon Beginning 4:44pm	Healing Leaf **14** Pisces Moon	Healing Leaf **15** Pisces Moon
Spring Flower **20** Gemini Moon	Spring Flower **21** Gemini Moon	Nurturing Leaf **22** Cancer Moon
Visible Roots **27** Virgo Moon	Visible Roots **28** Virgo Moon	Graceful Flower **29** Libra Moon

Graceful Flowers: Wines open gracefully, florals forward, guests slow to decide, patience. **Cactus Leaf:** Wines open gradually but deeply, guests will experience the wines emotionally. **Exotic Fruit:** Wines open enthusiastically, expect conversations to range far and wide.

Nurturing Leaf: Wines open slowly & voluptuously, help guests feel at home. **Abundant Fruit:** Wines open easily and generously, guests like to share their feelings about the wine. **Visible Roots:** Wines open carefully and thoughtfully, guests will want more info and details.

WEDNESDAY	THURSDAY	FRIDAY	SATURDAY
Graceful Flower **2** Libra Moon	Graceful Flower **3** Libra Moon	Cactus Leaf **4** Scorpio Moon	Cactus Leaf **5** Scorpio Moon
Climbing Root **9** Capricorn Moon	Full Moon Climbing Root **10** Capricorn Moon	Social Flower **11** Aquarius Moon Beginning 10:20am	Social Flower **12** Aquarius Moon
Bold Fruit **16** Aries Moon	Bold Fruit **17** Aries Moon	Grounded Root **18** Taurus Moon	Grounded Root **19** Taurus Moon
Nurturing Leaf **23** Cancer Moon	New Moon Abundant Fruit **24** Leo Moon	Abundant Fruit **25** Leo Moon	Visible Roots **26** Virgo Moon Beginning 1:55pm
Graceful Flower **30** Libra Moon	Cactus Leaf **31** Scorpio Moon		

Calculated for Pacific Clock Time

Climbing Root: Wines open slowly tannins forward, comments come when alcohol hits. **Social Flower:** Wines open broadly, esters forward, conversations take unexpected turns. **Healing Leaf:** Wines open patiently and dreamily, story telling and imagination soars.

July 1 through 6

TUESDAY 1	
WEDNESDAY 2	
THURSDAY 3	
FRIDAY 4	
SATURDAY 5	
SUNDAY 6	

July 7 through 13

	MONDAY 7
	TUESDAY 8
	WEDNESDAY 19
	THURSDAY 10
	FRIDAY 11
	SATURDAY 12
	SUNDAY 13

July 14 through 20

MONDAY 14	
TUESDAY 15	
WEDNESDAY 16	
THURSDAY 17	
FRIDAY 18	
SATURDAY 19	
SUNDAY 20	

July 21 through 27

	MONDAY 21
	TUESDAY 22
	WEDNESDAY 23
	THURSDAY 24
	FRIDAY 25
	SATURDAY 26
	SUNDAY 27

July 28 through 31

Monday 28	
Tuesday 29	
Wednesday 30	
Thursday 31	

10th - On this Full Moon, at 18 degrees Capricorn and Cancer, when you feel challenged, focus on the things you can control. It is going to be the little things where you will see progress. Look for where this is taking place in your chart because those areas will require some emotional discipline.

22nd - The Sun enters Leo, warming up the Charts, with the Moon in Cancer, so both are in Ruling Signs for a good couple of days to be out there in the world.

24th - The New Moon at 2 degrees Leo is cooperative rather than dynamic, so we come into the high summer with the need to attend to the simple things, and let the big stuff wait.

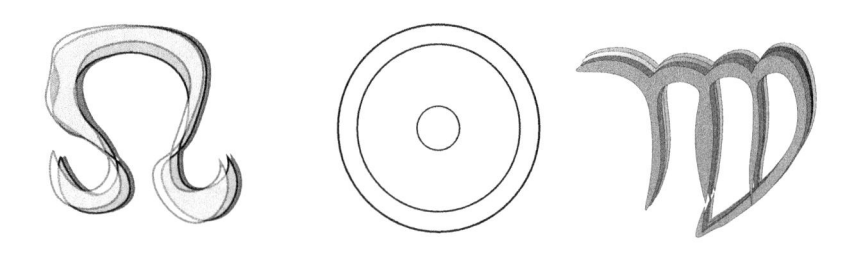

August Forecasts
Highlights from the Planetary Calendar
Leo the Lion to Virgo the Virgin

Astrologically this is a less complicated month, with most of the changes happening among the personal Planets, so be prepared to change your goals and directions and move onto the next stage. Mercury turning Direct on the 11th should smooth the waters although, be prepared for that New Moon on the 22nd, the day the Sun enters Virgo. This is the position of the star Regulus, the heart of the Lion. We point this out every year because it gives this period a lovely glow you should take the time to enjoy. As its position has moved from Tropical Leo into Tropical Virgo, better known as the Great Goddess, it is empowering the feminine, and this Lunation is all about that. Venus and Jupiter are in Cancer, the Sign of feminine Leadership. Mars is in the deeply personal position of Libra, the masculine Sign of Venus, that works especially well in home life.

Meanwhile, the Asteroids Vesta and Juno, the flame and the wife of Jupiter, are exactly Conjunct at 20 degrees Scorpio, the feminine Sign of Mars and a spot known for mental brilliance. The theme we see at this year of powerful women acting decisively at critical times continues this month. Forecast continues on page 70.

Bold Fruit: Wines open quickly, fruit forward, guests enthusiastically share opinions. **Grounded Root:** Wine open slowly but deliciously, don't rush and play pleasant music. **Spring Flowers:** Wines open quickly, acid forward, guests like to flirt and play games.

August 2025

Sunday	Monday	Tuesday
Exotic Fruit **31** Sagittarius Moon		
Exotic Fruit **3** Sagittarius Moon	Exotic Fruit **4** Sagittarius Moon	Climbing Root **5** Capricorn Moon
Healing Leaf **10** Pisces Moon	Healing Leaf **11** Pisces Moon	Bold Fruit **12** Aries Moon
Spring Flower **17** Gemini Moon	Nurturing Leaf **18** Cancer Moon Beginning 12:04pm	Nurturing Leaf **19** Cancer Moon
Visible Roots **24** Virgo Moon	Graceful Flower **25** Libra Moon	Graceful Flower **26** Libra Moon

Graceful Flowers: Wines open gracefully, florals forward, guests slow to decide, patience. **Cactus Leaf:** Wines open gradually but deeply, guests will experience the wines emotionally. **Exotic Fruit:** Wines open enthusiastically, expect conversations to range far and wide.

August 69

Nurturing Leaf: Wines open slowly & voluptuously, help guests feel at home. **Abundant Fruit:** Wines open easily and generously, guests like to share their feelings about the wine. **Visible Roots:** Wines open carefully and thoughtfully, guests will want more info and details.

WEDNESDAY	THURSDAY	FRIDAY	SATURDAY
		Cactus Leaf **1** Scorpio Moon	Cactus Leaf **2** Scorpio Moon
Climbing Root **6** Capricorn Moon	Climbing Root **7** Capricorn Moon	Social Flower **8** Aquarius Moon	Full Moon Social Flower **9** Aquarius Moon
Bold Fruit **13** Aries Moon	Grounded Root **14** Taurus Moon	Grounded Root **15** Taurus Moon	Spring Flower **16** Gemini Moon
Abundant Fruit **20** Leo Moon Beginning 4:16pm	Abundant Fruit **21** Leo Moon	New Moon Abundant Fruit **22** Leo Moon	Visible Roots **23** Virgo Moon
Graceful Flower **27** Libra Moon	Cactus Leaf **28** Scorpio Moon	Cactus Leaf **29** Scorpio Moon	Exotic Fruit **30** Sagittarius Moon

Calculated for Pacific Clock Time

Climbing Root: Wines open slowly tannins forward, comments come when alcohol hits. **Social Flower:** Wines open broadly, esters forward, conversations take unexpected turns. **Healing Leaf:** Wines open patiently and dreamily, story telling and imagination soars.

August 1 through 3

Virgo was originally called the Great Goddess because this was the time of year when the women would harvest the plants, most notably the grapes to make wine. The Constellation is the largest on the Ecliptic. She holds grapes in her left hand and a spike, or knife, for trimming the grapes in her right hand. The early Christian Astrologers wanted to destroy the Goddess' temples so they changed her knife into a stalk of wheat. They rebranded the Goddess, who was an artisan farmer and winemaker, into a helpless Virgin. But she is really the Goddess of Justice! **8th & 9th** - This Full Moon may be emotionally difficult, partly because a Mars opposed to Saturn can put people at loggerheads. With Jupiter at the Star Sirius and so close to Venus, find ways to finesse the issues by using your emotional intelligence.

22nd - The Sun enters Virgo at the New Moon at zero degrees Virgo, Conjunct the Star Regulus, the heart of the Lion. This is a powerful set point that speaks about the power of the Goddess.

FRIDAY
1

SATURDAY
2

SUNDAY
3

August 4 through 10

	MONDAY 4
	TUESDAY 5
	WEDNESDAY 6
	THURSDAY 7
	FRIDAY 8
	SATURDAY 9
	SUNDAY 10

August 11 through 17

MONDAY **11** Cactus Leaf	
TUESDAY **12**	
WEDNESDAY **13**	
THURSDAY **14**	
FRIDAY **15**	
SATURDAY **16**	
SUNDAY **17**	

August 18 through 24

	MONDAY 18
	TUESDAY 19
	WEDNESDAY 20
	THURSDAY 21
	FRIDAY 22
	SATURDAY 23
	SUNDAY 24

August 25 through 31

MONDAY 25	
TUESDAY 26	
WEDNESDAY 27	
THURSDAY 28	
FRIDAY 29	
SATURDAY 30	
SUNDAY 31	

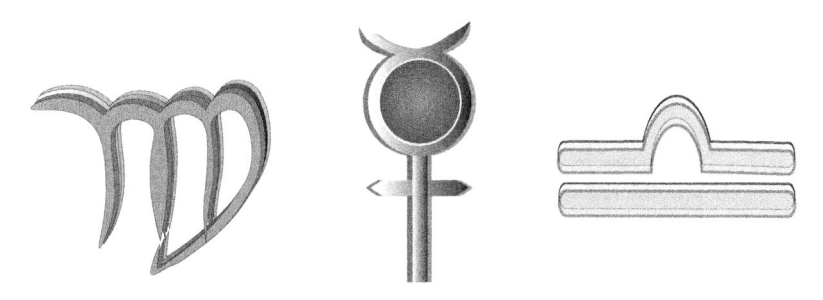

September Forecasts
Highlights from the Planetary Calendar
Virgo the Virgin to Libra the Scales

There is a great deal of Celestial activity this month, among both the Personal and Outer Planets. The BIG events are the two Eclipses, both involving Virgo on the 7th and 21st. There will be a strong sense of polarity between the personal and public lives, so focus on yourself because it will feel like outer events are beyond your control. You don't want to feel helpless! There is a fast Mercury so those tasks will move quickly and Venus entering Virgo turns the focus toward personal health. With Saturn, Uranus, Neptune and Pluto Retrograde, those outer affairs will feel stalled. But with Jupiter moving forward in Cancer commercial opportunities will improve, especially for home-based businesses and those focused on the home. But Jupiter will be turning Retrograde on the 11th of November so expect a slowdown then. When Saturn turns Direct later in the month, expect some commercial headwinds among conventional businesses. When Mars enters Scorpio, at the Equinox, its feminine Ruling Sign and the position of feminine power, be strategic. This is a good time to address difficult tasks connected to shared resources. The correct name for this Sign is the Eagle because it is patient and decisive. See where this is in your chart because there is power waiting there for you to access. People born in the Sign of the Eagle should drive very carefully during this Transit until the 4th of December. Forecast continues on page 82.

Bold Fruit: Wines open quickly, fruit forward, guests enthusiastically share opinions. **Grounded Root:** Wine open slowly but deliciously, don't rush and play pleasant music. **Spring Flowers:** Wines open quickly, acid forward, guests like to flirt and play games.

SEPTEMBER 2025

Sunday	Monday	Tuesday
	Exotic Fruit **1** Sagittarius Moon	Climbing Root **2** Capricorn Moon
Full Moon Eclipse Healing Leaf **7** Pisces Moon	Bold Fruit **8** Aries Moon Beginning 11:36am	Bold Fruit **9** Aries Moon
Spring Flower **14** Gemini Moon	Nurturing Leaf **15** Cancer Moon	Nurturing Leaf **16** Cancer Moon
New Moon Eclipse Graceful Flower **21** Libra Moon Beginning 2:40pm	Graceful Flower **22** Libra Moon	Graceful Flower **23** Libra Moon
Exotic Fruit **28** Sagittarius Moon	Climbing Root **29** Capricorn Moon	Climbing Root **30** Capricorn Moon

Graceful Flowers: Wines open gracefully, florals forward, guests slow to decide, patience. **Cactus Leaf:** Wines open gradually but deeply, guests will experience the wines emotionally. **Exotic Fruit:** Wines open enthusiastically, expect conversations to range far and wide.

September

Nurturing Leaf: Wines open slowly & voluptuously, help guests feel at home. **Abundant Fruit:** Wines open easily and generously, guests like to share their feelings about the wine. **Visible Roots:** Wines open carefully and thoughtfully, guests will want more info and details.

WEDNESDAY	THURSDAY	FRIDAY	SATURDAY
Climbing Root **3** Capricorn Moon	Social Flower **4** Aquarius Moon	Social Flower **5** Aquarius Moon	Healing Leaf **6** Pisces Moon
Grounded Root **10** Taurus Moon Beginning 1:03pm	Grounded Root **11** Taurus Moon	Spring Flower **12** Gemini Moon Beginning 2:38pm	Spring Flower **13** Gemini Moon
Abundant Fruit **17** Leo Moon	Abundant Fruit **18** Leo Moon	Visible Roots **19** Virgo Moon	Visible Roots **20** Virgo Moon
Cactus Leaf **24** Scorpio Moon	Cactus Leaf **25** Scorpio Moon	Exotic Fruit **26** Sagittarius Moon	Exotic Fruit **27** Sagittarius Moon

Calculated for Pacific Clock Time

Climbing Root: Wines open slowly tannins forward, comments come when alcohol hits. **Social Flower:** Wines open broadly, esters forward, conversations take unexpected turns. **Healing Leaf:** Wines open patiently and dreamily, story telling and imagination soars.

September 1 through 7

Monday 1	
Tuesday 2	
Wednesday 3	
Thursday 4	
Friday 5	
Saturday 6	
Sunday 7	

September 8 through 14

	MONDAY 8
	TUESDAY 9
	WEDNESDAY 10
	THURSDAY 11
	FRIDAY 12
	SATURDAY 13
	SUNDAY 14

September 15 through 21

MONDAY 15	
TUESDAY 16	
WEDNESDAY 17	
THURSDAY 18	
FRIDAY 19	
SATURDAY 20	
SUNDAY 21	

September 22 through 28

	MONDAY 22
	TUESDAY 23
	WEDNESDAY 24
	THURSDAY 25
	FRIDAY 26
	SATURDAY 27
	SUNDAY 28

September 29 through 30

Monday	
30	

Tuesday	
31	

7th - BOOM! The Total Lunar Eclipse at 15 degrees Pisces and Virgo may cause communication and infrastructure problems. Pisces and Virgo, pay attention because this impacts you emotionally and physically. Your intuition gets a jolt so take some longer walks to let your body process that. Everyone needs to pay attention to where this lands in your chart because it is being activated. The two weeks from now until the Solar Eclipse on the 21st may be emotionally difficult for some people so be kind and graceful.

21st - The Partial Solar Eclipse at 29 degrees Virgo at the New Moon, will likely be intense because the last degree of a Sign is the epitome of that energy. It opposes Saturn in Pisces and Neptune in Aries so there will be a powerful incentive to focus on your own well-being, because the great affairs of the world will seem to be 'way over there,' out of your control.

22nd - The Sun enters Libra at the Fall Equinox, leading Mercury and the Moon, and supported by Uranus. This is the same day that Mars enters the powerful Sign of Scorpio. It is a good time to seek partners in order to act because the days and nights are equally long and balanced.

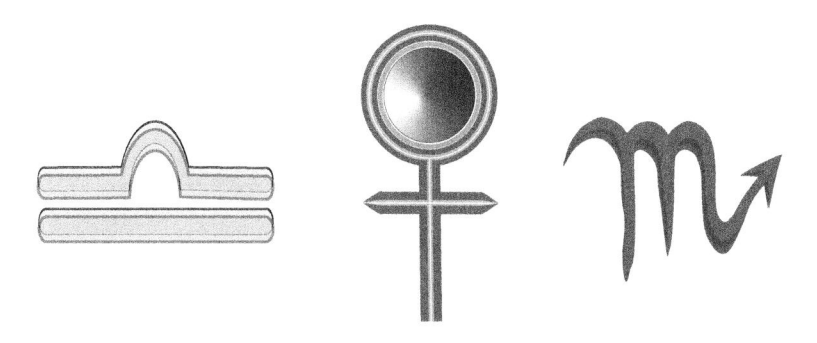

October Forecasts
Highlights from the Planetary Calendar
Libra the Scales to Scorpio the Scorpion

This is a less eventful Month that starts off a little unfocused, but the New Moon gets it on track. At this time of the year when the days are getting shorter, it is essential to recognize the best way to manage the resources you've gathered over the previous year. The sections on the New Moon and the Scorpio Ingress say it all. And there is a bonus piece about the meaning of Halloween!

6th - The Full Moon at 14 degrees Aries and Libra about twelve hours after Mercury enters Scorpio is filled with martial energy so watch your temper, tune out the static, and drive defensively.

21st – This is an extremely focused New Moon. There will be a sense that the players in the game are clearly identified. That's because Venus in Libra, Mars in Scorpio and Jupiter in Cancer are dignified Signs, two Rulers and one Exalted. They are clearly defined roles that work especially well in the world of career and public life. With Jupiter loosely Square the New Moon the conflict between businesses focused on personal gain, and what society considers fair will be highlighted. With Mercury Conjunct Mars, loosely Trine both Saturn and Jupiter, you can leverage your ideas very successfully. This is a great time to listen to the ideas of young people and harness that energy. Forecast continues pg 86.

Bold Fruit: Wines open quickly, fruit forward, guests enthusiastically share opinions. **Grounded Root:** Wine open slowly but deliciously, don't rush and play pleasant music. **Spring Flowers:** Wines open quickly, acid forward, guests like to flirt and play games.

OCTOBER 2025

SUNDAY	MONDAY	TUESDAY
Healing Leaf **5** Pisces Moon	Full Moon Bold Fruit **6** Aries Moon	Bold Fruit **7** Aries Moon
Nurturing Leaf **12** Cancer Moon	Nurturing Leaf **13** Cancer Moon	Abundant Fruit **14** Leo Moon
Graceful Flower **19** Libra Moon	Graceful Flower **20** Libra Moon	New Moon Cactus Leaf **21** Scorpio Moon
Climbing Root **26** Capricorn Moon	Climbing Root **27** Capricorn Moon	Climbing Root **28** Capricorn Moon

Graceful Flowers: Wines open gracefully, florals forward, guests slow to decide, patience. **Cactus Leaf:** Wines open gradually but deeply, guests will experience the wines emotionally. **Exotic Fruit:** Wines open enthusiastically, expect conversations to range far and wide.

Nurturing Leaf: Wines open slowly & voluptuously, help guests feel at home. **Abundant Fruit:** Wines open easily and generously, guests like to share their feelings about the wine. **Visible Roots:** Wines open carefully and thoughtfully, guests will want more info and details.

WEDNESDAY	THURSDAY	FRIDAY	SATURDAY
Social Flower **1** Aquarius Moon Beginning 12:51pm	Social Flower **2** Aquarius Moon	Social Flower **3** Aquarius Moon	Healing Leaf **4** Pisces Moon
Grounded Root **8** Taurus Moon	Grounded Root **9** Taurus Moon	Spring Flower **10** Gemini Moon	Spring Flower **11** Gemini Moon
Abundant Fruit **15** Leo Moon	Visible Roots **16** Virgo Moon	Visible Roots **17** Virgo Moon	Visible Roots **18** Virgo Moon
Cactus Leaf **22** Scorpio Moon	Cactus Leaf **23** Scorpio Moon	Exotic Fruit **24** Sagittarius Moon	Exotic Fruit **25** Sagittarius Moon
Social Flower **29** Aquarius Moon	Social Flower **30** Aquarius Moon	Healing Leaf **31** Pisces Moon	

Calculated for Pacific Clock Time

Climbing Root: Wines open slowly tannins forward, comments come when alcohol hits. **Social Flower:** Wines open broadly, esters forward, conversations take unexpected turns. **Healing Leaf:** Wines open patiently and dreamily, story telling and imagination soars.

October 1 through 5

22nd - The Sun enters Scorpio as Neptune backs into Pisces, joining the Moon, Mars and Mercury, so feminine power is strong now, strategize about difficult subjects and make decisions that will help your future.

Wednesday **1**	
Thursday **2**	
Friday **3**	
Saturday **4**	
Sunday **5**	

October 6 through 12

	MONDAY 6
	TUESDAY 7
	WEDNESDAY 8
	THURSDAY 9
	FRIDAY 10
	SATURDAY 11
	SUNDAY 12

October 13 through 19

MONDAY 13	
TUESDAY 14	
WEDNESDAY 15	
THURSDAY 16	
FRIDAY 17	
SATURDAY 18	
SUNDAY 19	

October 20 through 26

	MONDAY 20
	TUESDAY 21
	WEDNESDAY 22
	THURSDAY 23
	FRIDAY 24
	SATURDAY 25
	SUNDAY 26

October 27 through 31

MONDAY 27	
TUESDAY 28	
WEDNESDAY 29	
THURSDAY 30	
FRIDAY 31	

November Forecasts
Highlights from the Planetary Calendar
Scorpio the Scorpion to Sagittarius the Archer

This month is filled with Aspects, Ingresses and Changes. The first and third weeks are especially interesting, and potentially exciting. The big shift is Jupiter Turning Retrograde on the 11th and Saturn turning Direct on the 27th so the Bull Market will likely turn into a Bear as people focus on protecting their assets rather than risking them. But with so many Outer Planets Retrograde, global affairs will feel stymied. Scorpio and Sagittarius can be great times for the family and personal life, so focus on your personal wellbeing and tune out the news and noise.

5th - The Full Moon between Taurus and Scorpio may seem diffused because they are making few other Aspects. Planets in feminine Signs dominate so it's a responsive day rather than dynamic. Mercury and Mars in Sagittarius could add some levity to your home life.

19th - This is a chaotic New Moon opposite Uranus Conjunct the Pleiades while supported by loose Trines to Jupiter and Saturn. Emotional scars may resurface, but this is a time when you are empowered to address them from your experience and wisdom. Don't ignore this opportunity! Forecast continues on page 94.

Bold Fruit: Wines open quickly, fruit forward, guests enthusiastically share opinions. **Grounded Root:** Wine open slowly but deliciously, don't rush and play pleasant music. **Spring Flowers:** Wines open quickly, acid forward, guests like to flirt and play games.

NOVEMBER 2025

Sunday	Monday	Tuesday
Bold Fruit **30** Aries Moon		
Bold Fruit **2** Aries Moon	Bold Fruit **3** Aries Moon	Grounded Root **4** Taurus Moon
Nurturing Leaf **9** Cancer Moon	Abundant Fruit **10** Leo Moon	Abundant Fruit **11** Leo Moon
Graceful Flower **16** Libra Moon	Cactus Leaf **17** Scorpio Moon Beginning 1:44pm	Cactus Leaf **18** Scorpio Moon
Climbing Root **23** Capricorn Moon	Climbing Root **24** Capricorn Moon	Social Flower **25** Aquarius Moon

Graceful Flowers: Wines open gracefully, florals forward, guests slow to decide, patience. **Cactus Leaf:** Wines open gradually but deeply, guests will experience the wines emotionally. **Exotic Fruit:** Wines open enthusiastically, expect conversations to range far and wide.

November 2024

Nurturing Leaf: Wines open slowly & voluptuously, help guests feel at home. **Abundant Fruit:** Wines open easily and generously, guests like to share their feelings about the wine. **Visible Roots:** Wines open carefully and thoughtfully, guests will want more info and details.

Wednesday	Thursday	Friday	Saturday
			Healing Leaf **1** Pisces Moon
Full Moon Grounded Root **5** Taurus Moon	Spring Flower **6** Gemini Moon	Spring Flower **7** Gemini Moon	Nurturing Leaf **8** Cancer Moon
Visible Roots **12** Virgo Moon Beginning 3:51pm	Visible Roots **13** Virgo Moon	Visible Roots **14** Virgo Moon	Graceful Flower **15** Libra Moon
New Moon Cactus Leaf **19** Scorpio Moon	Exotic Fruit **20** Sagittarius Moon	Exotic Fruit **21** Sagittarius Moon	Climbing Root **22** Capricorn Moon Beginning 2:52pm
Social Flower **26** Aquarius Moon	Healing Leaf **27** Pisces Moon Beginning 11:23am	Healing Leaf **28** Pisces Moon	Healing Leaf **29** Pisces Moon

Calculated for Pacific Clock Time

Climbing Root: Wines open slowly tannins forward, comments come when alcohol hits. **Social Flower:** Wines open broadly, esters forward, conversations take unexpected turns. **Healing Leaf:** Wines open patiently and dreamily, story telling and imagination soars.

November 1st through 2

21st - The Sun enters Sagittarius, joining Mars and the Moon, so it will feel like the page suddenly turned and things lightened up. Symbolically, this is the time after the Fall wind knocks the last of the leaves off the trees and the vistas suddenly expand. With the Sun making Aspects to Uranus and Neptune, there will be a widescale sense of the hidden designs suddenly becoming visible. Time to order your 2026 Lunar Tasting Calendar.

SATURDAY 1

SUNDAY 2

November 3 through 9

	MONDAY 3
	TUESDAY 4
	WEDNESDAY 5
	THURSDAY 6
	FRIDAY 7
	SATURDAY 8
	SUNDAY 9

November 10 through 16

MONDAY 10	
TUESDAY 11	
WEDNESDAY 12	
THURSDAY 13	
FRIDAY 15	
SATURDAY 15	
SUNDAY 16	

November 17 through 23

	MONDAY 17
	TUESDAY 18
	WEDNESDAY 19
	THURSDAY 20
	FRIDAY 21
	SATURDAY 22
	SUNDAY 23

November 24 through 30

MONDAY 24	
TUESDAY 25	
WEDNESDAY 26	
THURSDAY 27	
FRIDAY 28	
SATURDAY 29	
SUNDAY 30	

December Forecasts
Highlights from the Planetary Calendar
Sagittarius the Archer to Capricorn the Sea Goat

Optimistic Jupiter usually holds sway over December because the Sun spends the first twenty days of the month in Sagittarius. This is the Planet's dynamic career Sign, known for expansiveness, generosity, scholarship, and a love of foreign places. So, that's when we go searching for gifts from far-away places to share with those we care about. That's why our favorite scents and flavors of this season, like cinnamon and allspice, come from tropical islands on the other side of the Earth. *This year, Jupiter is especially in command because the three dominant Signs are Sagittarius, Pisces and Cancer, where we find Jupiter.* These are the Planet's two Ruling 'Career' Signs and its Exalted 'Colleague' Sign. These are the three positions where the Planet's energy functions best in public life. Even after the Sun enters Capricorn at the Winter Solstice, its ruling Planet Saturn, is in Pisces, the Feminine Ruling 'Career' Sign of Jupiter, so that influence continues. *Because Jupiter is in Cancer, it's connected to the Moon, and to a lesser extent the Sun.* So, expect the first part of the month to be especially variable, with plenty of movement, getting things done in an intuitive, instinctive way. Once the Sun enters Capricorn it will feel more serious, but with Mercury and Venus still in Sagittarius, a certain lightness will remain. Forecast continues on page 106.

Bold Fruit: Wines open quickly, fruit forward, guests enthusiastically share opinions. **Grounded Root:** Wine open slowly but deliciously, don't rush and play pleasant music. **Spring Flowers:** Wines open quickly, acid forward, guests like to flirt and play games.

DECMBER 2025

SUNDAY	MONDAY	TUESDAY
	Bold Fruit **1** Aries Moon	Grounded Root **2** Taurus Moon
Nurturing Leaf **7** Cancer Moon	Abundant Fruit **8** Leo Moon	Abundant Fruit **9** Leo Moon
Graceful Flower **14** Libra Moon	Cactus Leaf **15** Scorpio Moon	Cactus Leaf **16** Scorpio Moon
Climbing Root **21** Capricorn Moon	Social Flower **22** Aquarius Moon	Social Flower **23** Aquarius Moon
Bold Fruit **28** Aries Moon	Grounded Root **29** Taurus Moon	Grounded Root **30** Taurus Moon

Graceful Flowers: Wines open gracefully, florals forward, guests slow to decide, patience. **Cactus Leaf:** Wines open gradually but deeply, guests will experience the wines emotionally. **Exotic Fruit:** Wines open enthusiastically, expect conversations to range far and wide.

December 2024   101

Nurturing Leaf: Wines open slowly & voluptuously, help guests feel at home. **Abundant Fruit:** Wines open easily and generously, guests like to share their feelings about the wine. **Visible Roots:** Wines open carefully and thoughtfully, guests will want more info and details.

WEDNESDAY	THURSDAY	FRIDAY	SATURDAY
Grounded Root **3** Taurus Moon	Full Moon Spring Flower **4** Gemini Moon	Spring Flower **5** Gemini Moon	Nurturing Leaf **6** Cancer Moon
Visible Roots **10** Virgo Moon	Visible Roots **11** Virgo Moon	Graceful Flower **12** Libra Moon	Graceful Flower **13** Libra Moon
Exotic Fruit **17** Sagittarius Moon	Exotic Fruit **18** Sagittarius Moon	New Moon Exotic Fruit **19** Sagittarius Moon	Climbing Root **20** Capricorn Moon
Social Flower **24** Aquarius Moon	Healing Leaf **25** Pisces Moon	Healing Leaf **26** Pisces Moon	Bold Fruit **27** Aries Moon
Spring Flower **31** Gemini Moon			

Calculated for Pacific Clock Time

Climbing Root: Wines open slowly tannins forward, comments come when alcohol hits. **Social Flower:** Wines open broadly, esters forward, conversations take unexpected turns. **Healing Leaf:** Wines open patiently and dreamily, story telling and imagination soars.

December 1 through 7

MONDAY 1	
TUESDAY 2	
WEDNESDAY 3	
THURSDAY 4	
FRIDAY 5	
SATURDAY 6	
SUNDAY 7	

December 8 through 14

	MONDAY **8**
	TUESDAY **9**
	WEDNESDAY **10**
	THURSDAY **11**
	FRIDAY **12**
	SATURDAY **13**
	SUNDAY **14**

December 15 through 21

MONDAY 15	
TUESDAY 16	
WEDNESDAY 17	
THURSDAY 18	
FRIDAY 19	
SATURDAY 20	
SUNDAY 21	

December 22 through 28

	MONDAY 22
	TUESDAY 23
	WEDNESDAY 24
	THURSDAY 25
	FRIDAY 26
	SATURDAY 27
	SUNDAY 28

December 29 through 31

MONDAY 29	
TUESDAY 30	
WEDNESDAY 31	*Remember to get your 2026 Calendar.*

4th - The Moon opposes Venus, just before the Full Moon at 13 degrees Gemini and Sagittarius. The lunation isn't getting much support or structure from the other Planets. So, expect to feel less pressure to get things done, and be more inclined to focus on your relationships until the New Moon on the 19th. This is not a bad strategy to pursue in December!

19th - At the New Moon at 28 degrees Sagittarius, the theme of focusing on people rather than ideas or jobs continues. There will be a very obvious balancing act between those who are optimistic and the worriers. Be prepared for unexpected events, climatic or financial, happening close to the New Moon thanks to an exact Quincunx to Uranus in Taurus.

21st - At the Winter Solstice, the shortest days of the year, the Sun moves into Capricorn joining Mars. The Sun in Capricorn is a deeply personal position, but the Mars in Capricorn is very social so be prepared to stay true to yourself, while showing up for everyone else.

Chapter One

Timing Wine Tastings by the Moon

Anyone who does tastings often, whether for work, or simply to enjoy the flavors of the world, may have noticed that wines seem to react differently depending on the day. In the Biodynamic approach to organic viticulture, winemakers use an astrological calendar to time events, including for conducting tastings. Based on their experiences they prefer certain Moon Signs for wine tastings, especially their commercial events.

After attending thousands of tastings with clients we've noticed that the Moon Sign does make a difference. But we have also noticed that every day seems to be good for wine tasting, just in different ways. If you work in the wine industry, the suggestions we offer here, can help you more consistently produce excellent experiences for your customers and hopefully better sales.

If you are a wine enthusiast, it can help you gain a great deal of insight and enjoyment from the wine. As we explain, this if we lean towards the experiences of the winery tasting rooms please forgive us, because that is where we learned about how people and wines react during the various Moon Signs.

The key to using this is knowing the Moon's current 'Element' at the time of the tasting. This simplifies the system, because while there are twelve astrology Signs, they each belong to one of the four Elements. These are not the elements from the scientific periodic table developed in the 1800's.

Instead, this is the original definition of the word 'Element', meaning the forces of nature, Fire, Earth, Air and Water, which modern science calls the four states of matter, Plasma, Solid, Gaseous and Liquid. *The Moon goes through the twelve Signs in about twenty-eight days, changing Sign, and Element, every two and a half days.*

The Signs are divided into Elements in this order. The Horoscope traditionally starts with **Spring**:
Aries the Ram is a Fire Sign, Taurus is Earth, Gemini is Air,
Then **Summer:**
Cancer the Crab is Water, Leo is Fire, Virgo is Earth,
Then **Autumn:**
Libra the Scales is Air, Scorpio is Water, Sagittarius is Fire,
Then **Winter:**
Capricorn the Sea Lion is Earth, Aquarius is Air, Pisces is Water.

The Moon's Element affects the tasting in two ways. First, it determines how quickly the wines mix with oxygen, releasing their bouquet and flavors. Second, it reveals what will be most appealing about the experience!

The Element Biodynamic wineries prefer for industry tastings is Fire, which includes Aries, Leo and Sagittarius. During Fire Moons the wines open quickly and create a strong first impression with the fruit flavors. The Air Element is the second choice. While the wines also open quickly, they tend to emphasize the floral notes and alcohol content. On Earth and Water Moons the wines open slowly, and while Earth brings out the earthy and woody flavors, Water enhances any vegetal flavors in the wine.

Obviously, in winery tasting rooms, the hosts don't get to choose the Moon Sign when their clients decide to visit. Fortunately, the experience is about more than just their first impression of the wine. There are numerous factors affecting a guest's enjoyment that the host can finesse when they work with the day's Moon theme!

Here are Examples of What We Mean!

Clue #1. We've all picked up a glass of wine and smelled it, doing our best to understand the message in that bouquet. The nose can detect almost a billion scents, including some in wine that are only released when the liquid touches the bacteria on the tongue. When the palate reads the flavors, the body creates enzymes to take advantage of those nutrients which are called flavors. That's why a well-made wine makes the body 'feel better' with the first sip. Fire Moons accentuate the nose and palate experience, and excel at promoting quick, sensory engagement.

Clue #2. Marketing experts had long advised wineries, with little success, to abandon their tastings bars in favor of doing seated sessions because it improves sales. Then the shutdown forced them into doing outdoor seated tastings. Guess what? With fewer customers and higher tasting fees sales improved! On Air Moons people enjoy the discussion and social interaction that happens more naturally around a table, elevating the tasting experience and overall enjoyment.

Clue #3. One winery that only offered food pairings as an option noticed that those paired tastings consistently sold more than the wines offered on their own. So, they expanded their kitchen so they could include a pairing with every tasting. On Earth Moons the savory flavors in food wake up the palate, and brings out the best in the wine, including the wood flavors like vanilla and chocolate, always favorites, helping the guest associate it with foods the wine would go well with.

Clue #4. The host's personality dramatically affects sales. Charming tasting room superstars combine friendliness, sales skills and knowledge of their wines to deliver experiences which their customers remember for years, while maximizing sales and club memberships. On Water Moons people need to feel welcome and accepted because they want an emotional connection with the winery. Telling them engaging stories about the makers and the place shapes their experience of the wine. A great host makes the wines seem sweeter, but with a grumpy host…you can just imagine!

Clearly, there's more to the tasting experience than just the wine! That's why sales strategies and a particular type of pairing may work well for a couple of days, but run into a wall on the third, when the Moon changes Elements! The secret is to adjust your approach with the 'tides'.

Insights About the Fire and Air Moons

During these Moon Signs the wine quickly mixes with oxygen, releasing its aromas. A person's experience of the wine is immediate and focused on the nose and the sense of smell. This strongly informs and colors their experience of the juice. Because the experience is more in the eyes, nose and the frontal brain, food pairings should be minimized so they don't distract from the encounter.

On Fruit/Fire days the fruit stands out which is often preferred with red wines. On Air Days the floral notes carried by the alcohol become more evident, so that benefits delicate white wines.

On Flower/Air Moons be careful with high alcohol wines because the fumes can obscure the flavors. It is important to use large glasses, tilting them almost horizontal to let the fumes rise inside the bowl and escape at the top lip like a chimney. Then place the nose on the lower lip, below the alcohol fumes, where the heavier bouquet of the fruit resides.

Insights About the Earth and Water Moons

During these Moons the aromas are tightly bound in the liquid, so it takes longer with more aggressive swirling to get the flavors to reveal themselves. The initial impression via the nose is less dramatic than on the Fire and Air Moons. Instead, the flavor experience is concentrated on the palate, connected to the limbic part of the brain where emotions live. Stretch out the tasting and lead your guests through properly aerating the wine and pushing the juice into the nooks and crannies of the palate, so the full gamut of flavors can be experienced. Food pairings complementing the wine with savory notes are especially helpful.

The Root/Earth Moons show off the deeper phenolic flavors emerging from the roots and wood. Pairings with a flavor profile that combine mostly savory, with and a little bit sweet, compliment those woody flavors best. Also, the guest's physical comfort is paramount for keeping them in their seat long enough for the wines to fully express themselves, so position them carefully. Earth Moons are practical days and the more you emphasize the benefits of wine, of which there are many to both the body and the soul, the better.

The Leaf/Water Moons bring out vegetal flavors so it's important to choose wines that don't contain notes of green pepper or asparagus that emerge when the grapes were not fully ripe. Adding cheese to the pairing optimizes the flavors on Water days. The important part is that everyone at the tasting feels welcome and accepted. With Water more than any other element, those positive emotional connections will affect the chemistry of the body and make the wine taste better. The key on Water Moons is embodied in the customer service saying, *"People may forget what you did for them, but they will always remember how you made them feel"* Offer your guests water and encourage them to stay hydrated, telling them that the alcohol should spread throughout their body until even their feet feel good, and their heads feel light! That simple effort shows that you care about them which is the secret on Water Moons.

Using the Moon's position related to the four elements is the easiest and quickest way to make this work. But be aware, each Sign affects the experience in a unique way, so we provided a **Moon Sign Reference Key at the beginning of the book** with ideas about how to create the best possible experience for your guests and yourself during each Moon Sign!

Following this chapter is one from the Planetary Calendar's companion book the explains the Astrological Signs in more detail. Following that is a chapter from our Tour Books that looks at some of wine tasting techniques.

Chapter Two: Fine Wine and the Planets

"Wine is sunlight held together by water" - Galileo Galilei

In 1811 the "Great Comet" was visible for over eight months, and the year's wine was called a "Comet Vintage". That year's flawless Château d'Yquem enjoyed exceptional longevity, the Veuve Clicquot was heralded as the first 'modern' Champagne and while 1811 stands out, all of the 'comet vintages' are believed exceptional.

Our consulting spans both Astrology and wine tourism, places where the history of natural cycles rule, so we divide our time talking with clients about their Planets and the vineyards that produce the wines they like. A person's wine preferences are often expressions of their Charts, accounting for differences in age, economic status, education, gender and physiology. Personal transits affect what appeals to their palates and the travel experiences people seek. Saturn Transits often inspire wine trips to Bordeaux, with all their formality and tradition. Jupiter Transits more often lead to bouncing among the California vineyards, with the hospitable, over-blown and entrepreneurial style. Three factors shape wine preferences; personality, physiology and age. Astrologically, Personality is the Sun and Moon, Physiology is the Ascendant and Age is seen in the transits. Older men and Saturnian personalities like big, structured, aged Reds. Youngsters, before their Saturn Return at the age of twenty-eight, often like lighter, even sweeter wines that delight and excite the front of the palette. As people age the flavors that appeal to them are sensed farther back on the palate. After the Saturn Return, the mid-palette, savory flavors of calcium, magnesium, sodium and potassium become more appealing. At that critical juncture the body's ability to assimilate these nutrients is reduced, so it becomes increasingly important that the body seek them out.

Herbalists have traditionally made correlations between plants and Planets. With grapes that's easy, because they look like Celestial Bodies, round, colorful with distinctive personalities. Having our unique perspective, we looked for correlations between the major Planets and the grapes that dominate the 'fine wine' world.

Here is a helpful hint for wine lovers from Biodynamics, the oldest, 'modern' system of organic farming, that includes an Astrological system. Wine is more fragrant and tastes better during Fire and Air Moons, compared to Water and Earth Moons. That's because the flavors volatize more easily under those Moons.

A major part of the sensory enjoyment of wine is through the nose, which can detect almost a billion scent notes, while the palate only gets five major flavors. We have noticed this ourselves and the Moon Sign is an important factor for when the great Biodynamic French wine houses schedule their industry tasting events.

The Celestial Bodies and Their Grapes

The Sun – Chardonnay. When that golden glass of Chardonnay is glowing in the café light you are seeing the embodiment of the Sun. The name in Persian means 'The Gates of Heaven', and as befits the Sun, Chard is America's biggest selling premium white wine; climate tolerant, insect resistant, prolific and able to be made in many styles. Like all grapes, they start off green but as they attain ripeness, they become a translucent gold, with subtle sunspots floating beneath the surface. That vitality and adaptability is clearly Solar.

The Moon – Moscato. This grape is a large golden globe, a touch speckled and sometimes colored a soft rose all over; fragrant, watery and inclined to a high sugar level. How feminine and Lunar is that? Doubling as a table grape, it's a special seasonal treat.

Inside the winery Moscato flashes multiple faces, from its famous sweet wine, to a bright, dry glass that still retains its trace of perfume. It likes to be part of a family and is often mixed with other wines to add some 'nose' and softness, especially with stiff Chardonnay and the Mercurial Pinot Blanc, to create what the French call their White Burgundy.

Mercury - Pinot Noir and Pinot Blanc are the two faces of Mercury, small, delicate grapes growing beside Solar Chardonnay. The name 'Pinot', for the 'Pine' cone shaped bunches, the source of pine nuts, makes sense because these grapes drive growers nuts, with their challenges; something they have in common with Mercury ruled people.

Pinot Blanc is rarely made as a single wine. A bit thin in personality, it has the wonderful ability to reflect and complement another grape's gifts with those famous Gemini engaging skills. Even Pinot Noir, which is made as a single grape, is often a mix of various 'clones' or mutations from varied vineyards, like a troupe of Virgos, working together to accomplish a task.

As easy as Chard is to grow, the Pinot twins are more troublesome, thin-skinned, sensitive to everything and even at their best, their yields, like their berries and the Planet Mercury, are small.

Venus – Riesling. Few wines bring a smile to the lips as quickly as Riesling because of its light body, bright fragrance and sweet flavor, it often appeals to younger palates. For many people this grape from the northlands is the first glass that opened their eyes to the possibilities of wine. How much like Venus is that, the power of love, beauty and attraction to make you notice something that you had, up until then, overlooked.

Growing Riesling is a labor of love because it thrives in very specific locations where other grapes would not. Like all grapes, it needs plenty of sunlight, but its thin, light-colored skin lets it ripen quicker than most. To grow a good Riesling in these cooler climates, they pick the warmest spots with the most sunshine; steep, terraced, southern facing hillside vineyards overlooking the river. The amount of effort and care required for those remarkable locations seems out of proportion to their results, but that's what people will do for the sake of Venus.

Mars – Malbec. The connection between Mars and hormones is clear, because both are powerful, sociable, sure to get your attention, but short lived. Interestingly, according to Biodynamics Mars is considered the most important Planet for growing grapes because of their similar ruddy complexions, as most grapes are red. Malbec possesses a rich flavor, great color, but low tannins, which makes it a favorite with women, fitting perfectly with Mars Ruled Scorpio, the Sign of strong women.

Even though Mars is Earth's neighbor, it is half the size of Venus and twice as far from Earth. That is like Malbec, which historically comes from the small Cohors Valley, to the east of the much larger, richer Bordeaux region. But small is still potent and the 'Black Wine of Cohors' was especially prized by the ancient Romans and Czarist Russia, two Martial societies.

Jupiter – Merlot. The big, juicy Merlot berry makes a richly flavored, well-rounded wine with fruity flavors, but very low amounts of the tannins that pucker your lips. This sounds so much like how we describe the abundantly appealing nature of huge Jupiter. Merlot became an early favorite when single varietal wines became popular because the flavors opened and became accessible quickly and it went well with so many foods.

Like Jupiter's two Signs, Sagittarius and Pisces, Merlot is a very social wine and an early favorite in the bar scene. That's because 'Merlot' was easier to pronounce in front of a young lady than Cabernet Sauvignon, Sangiovese or Gewürztraminer.

Merlot's burgeoning popularity produced too much mediocre wine, until the movie 'Sideways', where the main character rails against the grape, dramatically damaging sales. That was like the comet Hale Bopp slamming into Jupiter! But Merlot, like Jove, is hard to keep down and Merlot's quality and popularity, thanks to better vineyard strategies, has gradually rebounded.

Saturn – Cabernet Sauvignon. Saturn is the old man of the ancient Planets, taking twenty-eight years to orbit the Sun and Cabernet is one of the last vines to flower, the last to harvest and the more time it has on the vines and in the bottle the better it tastes. Cab loves the sun, dry weather and well-drained soils, high in sulfur, to make tannins that give Cabernet its ability to survive in the cellars.

That Saturnian durability is why it commands high prices. It is the banker's wine because you put it in your cellar and it increases in value, year after year. Buy a Cabernet the year a child is born and enjoy it with them on their twenty-first birthday, or better yet, at their Saturn Return.

Cabernets, like Saturn with its spectacular rings, is renowned for its beauty, sporting deeply colored reds with a flickering of other hues as the glass's level descends. While young people find those tannins and complex flavors overwhelming, older men, with less sensitive, but more experienced palettes, appreciate the strongly structured flavors that their bodies crave.

Uranus – Viognier. Both the Planet and the Wine make deceptive first impressions. Uranus was long mistaken for a Star until the 1700's when it was revealed as a Planet. But then, Surprise! Its odd nature was revealed. Unlike the other Planets that stand upright, spinning like a top, Uranus rotates on its East-West axis, sailing through space like a well thrown football.

Viognier also surprises because its floral scent doesn't foretell the structured, full-bodied wine on your palette. Uranus is the only planet beyond Saturn, that given ideal conditions, can be seen without a telescope. Viognier had almost died out but was rescued from obscurity by the Central Coast winemakers seeking "ABC wines", for people who want "Anything But Chardonnay", that would thrive in their cool, windy hills. Uranus is also considered the Alternative Planet. Those winemakers were so tired of making tank after tank of Chardonnay that the alternative, Viognier, even though difficult and demanding to make, was a welcome change.

Neptune – Zinfandel. The Planet and the Wine are both mysterious, often defying description and are favorites in California. With the state's long Pacific coastline and spectacular harbors, Neptune, the God of the Seas, clearly holds sway. Zinfandel was long thought a 'native' Californian grape, an emotion that persists despite genetic testing claims from coastal Croatia, but with Neptune, feelings matter more than facts! Neptune's influence is nebulous, acting behind the scenes, it is associated with the imagination, alcohol and drugs, and it is an important 'money' Planet.

That's like Zinfandel, it has an unusual combination of qualities; both full body and deep color, but the grapes are early ripening, so it comes to the market early. That's why Zin was so popular during Prohibition, when tons of grapes were shipped to the big East Coast cities, the earlier your grapes made it to the train yards, the better chance you had of selling every bunch. Zin is often made in a very intoxicating, high alcohol version.

Like Neptune, Zin often lives in the background, a durable vine, whose deep roots are hidden from view. Its grapes are often included, but unacknowledged, in inexpensive red blends. Neptune also travels beyond the reach of the naked eye, ruling those who make movies, video games and wine, so just like Zinfandel, Neptune is perfectly at home in the Virgo Ruled Golden State.

Pluto - Petite Verdot. This is the small, dark grape, whose name means 'The little green one'. It is mostly added to red Bordeaux blends to replace tannins and colors washed out of the Cabernet grapes by early rains. Without those components the wine won't age properly. It is rarely made by itself, but fermented alone it is a profoundly dark, appealing red wine. That is so like Pluto, a Planet smaller than Earth's Moon, but with five Moons of its own, invisible to the naked eye, traveling on its long Solar orbit through the depths of space.

It adds depth and intensity to the chart through its Conjunctions with other Planets. Petite Verdot also has a long timeline, ripening late in the season, and making its invisible presence known by helping the wines extend their lives years into the future. Pluto, thanks to its long orbit, is also about the historical perspective. It teaches us about the purposes and limitations of power, a lesson that is most often learned later in life.

Wine is one of the proofs that God
loves us and wants us to be happy
- Benjamin Franklin, Astrologer and Statesman
Well said Ben!

2025

**Planetary Calendar
Day Planner**

**& Astrology Forecasts
Calculated for Pacific Time**

Moon Signs, VOC, Phases, Eclipses
Planetary Positions & Retrogrades
Meteor Showers
Holidays & Much More
For Students & Experts

Tracking the Planets Since 1949

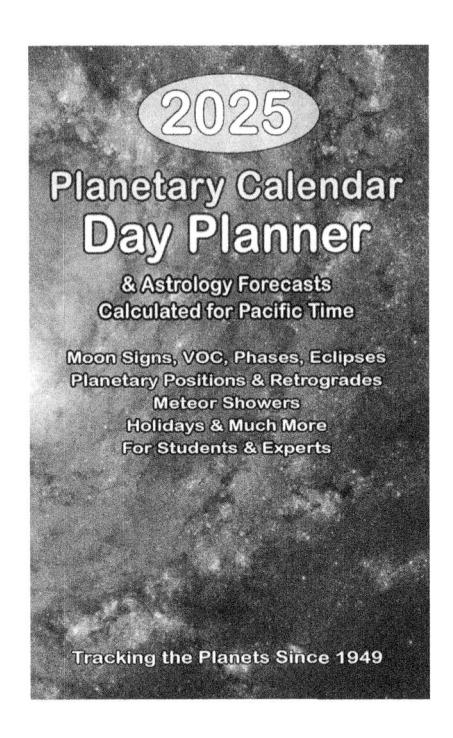

Chapters Two & Six are from the

'Planetary Calendar with Astrology Forecasts'
produced since 1949 and available as
wall, pocket, day planner and digital versions.

Chapter Two expands on the segment
'The Best Days for Wine Tasting'.

Chapter Six, The Calendar pages,
shows the Moon's location daily by Sign.

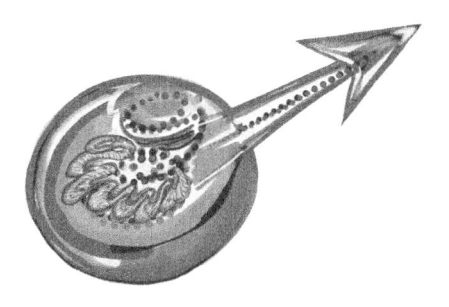

Chapter Three: The Signs as Actions

Almost everyone knows their Sun Sign, or where the Sun was in their chart when they were born. But, do they understand that the twelve Signs describe thirty-degree sections of the path in the sky, called the Ecliptic, where the Sun appears to travel, one degree each day, creating the year?

Because the Ecliptic and Equator are not parallel, but cross at a 23-degree angle, the Sun splits it time between the northern and southern hemispheres, creating the seasons.

The first day of each season is a turning point in the Sun's yearly passage, which most importantly, we experience through the changing length of the day. On the first days of Spring (Vernal Equinox, 1st degree Aries) and Fall (Autumnal Equinox, 1st degree Libra), when the Sun crosses the Equator, the day and night are equal length.

After the Vernal Equinox (Equal Night) each day is longer, until the first day of Summer (Summer Solstice, 1st degree of Cancer). After the Autumnal Equinox each day is shorter, until the first day of Winter (Winter Solstice, 1st Capricorn). What all this means is that the Signs represent time, location and the angle with which the Earth is receiving the Sun's light!

Understanding the Connections Between the Signs

Each season is a quarter segment of that Ecliptic pathway, and each segment is divided into three sections, which are the Signs. The shifting angle of the light in the Sun's apparent annual journey, and its effects on weather, determine the actions that take place during each period. Each thirty-degree Sign builds upon what happened before. For example, during the last third of Winter, Pisces, the thaw makes dissolved nutrients available to the sprouting plants, encouraged to the surface by the warming of Spring, in Aries.

The twelve Signs are equal components in that cycle, related to each other by four criteria that are unique to time and Astrology; Season, Polarity, Element and Quality. This is a little like the four familial connections that humans make to their parents, siblings, mates and children.

First, What is the Sign's Season: Are they part of Spring, Summer, Fall or Winter? Spring is the season of hope, Summer is the season of fulfillment, Fall is the season of consolidation and Winter is the season of contraction.

The Polarities

Second, What is The Sign's Polarity? Traditionally the Signs are considered masculine or feminine, alternately, Yang or Yin. But we prefer Dynamic or Receptive, because that describes their action rather than their nature. The Signs start with Dynamic Aries, then Receptive Taurus, Dynamic Gemini, Receptive Cancer, Dynamic Leo, Receptive Virgo, Dynamic Libra, Receptive Scorpio, Dynamic Sagittarius, Receptive Capricorn, Dynamic Aquarius, Receptive Pisces. This tells you whether the energy is Dynamically pushing into the social world or Receptively pulling into the personal world.

Third, What is The Sign's Element? Many people know the four traditional elements that come to us through the ancient Greeks, Fire, Earth, Air and Water. This is not equivalent to our modern Elemental Table, denoting Oxygen, Hydrogen, Zinc, etc. Those ancient elements describe what modern science calls the four states of Matter: Fire equals Plasma, Earth equals Solid, Air equals Gas and Water equals Liquid. The Element describes the Sign's essential 'being' and the way they act in the world. Each Sign within an Element shares that essential nature although they will express it differently depending on their season.

For example, the Summer Water Sign Cancer operates very differently from the Winter Sign Pisces, because warm water in the summer and cold water in the winter are experienced very differently. That ocean you would happily play in during the Summer looks remarkably uninviting in the Winter. Each Sign of an Element is separated by 120 degrees. In Astrology this Aspect is called a Trine and it is considered a supportive, harmonious relationship.

The Fire Signs are Aries, Leo and Sagittarius. The Earth Signs are Taurus, Virgo and Capricorn. The Air Signs are Gemini, Libra and Aquarius. The Water Signs are Cancer, Scorpio and Pisces.

About the Chinese "Elements"

The concept of the Chinese 'Elements' has caused all kinds of confusion due to a mistranslation because the concept sounded similar, but the Western and Asian 'Elements' describe two different systems. As we stated, the Western system, which is also used by Indian Astrologers (Vedic) describes the States of Matter. The proper translation for the Chinese concept is 'Stages'. But please don't confuse that with the stages of the seasons that we just discussed. What the Chinese are talking about are the physiological actions of the Planets as described in the body.

This is a basic tenant of Chinese medicine. When you experience an event, physical, emotional or mental, it is processed by Planet after Planet, body system after system, until its influence on you is done. Most life events are handled routinely. But some events are traumatic, and that trip down the production line is rocky. That is why 'letting go' of an event is often the path to feeling better. Disease occurs when the event lands in one of those stages and gets stuck there.

Chinese medicine is about getting that process flowing again, by energizing or relaxing the correct body systems, and each relates to a Planet. There are five systems or stages; Metal (Mercury), Moon (Water), Wood (Saturn), Fire (Jupiter) and Earth (Venus). These are modulated by two qualities, Heart Warmth (Sun) and Hormonal Heat (Mars). That makes seven players; that is the same number as the traditional Western Planets that they describe. Read Chapter 15 to learn more about the Chinese approach to Astrology and healing.

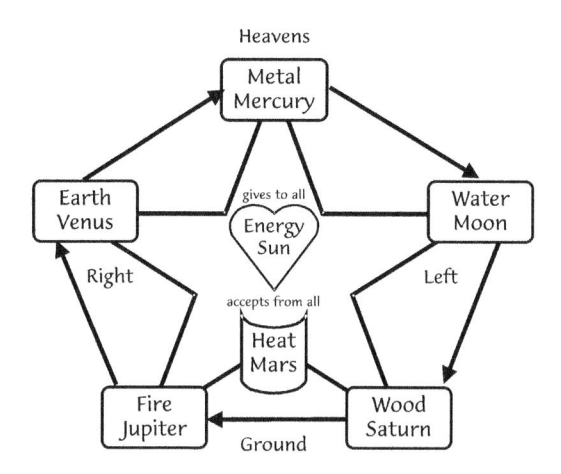

```
                    Heavens
                  ┌─────────┐
                  │  Metal  │
                  │ Mercury │
                  └─────────┘
     ┌───────┐    gives to all    ┌───────┐
     │ Earth │    ┌────────┐      │ Water │
     │ Venus │    │ Energy │      │ Moon  │
     └───────┘    │  Sun   │      └───────┘
       Right      └────────┘        Left
                 accepts from all
                  ┌────────┐
                  │  Heat  │
                  │  Mars  │
                  └────────┘
     ┌───────┐                    ┌────────┐
     │ Fire  │                    │  Wood  │
     │Jupiter│                    │ Saturn │
     └───────┘                    └────────┘
                    Ground
```

Fourth: What is their Quality? We can also define this as the Sign's 'standing' or 'positioning' because it is determined by the Sign's placement within its season. They are Cardinal, Fixed and Mutable. The Cardinal Signs are Aries, Cancer, Libra and Capricorn. The Fixed Signs are Taurus, Leo, Scorpio and Aquarius. The Mutable Signs are Gemini, Virgo, Sagittarius and Pisces.

The first 30 degrees of each season are the Cardinal Signs. They take action. The next 30 degrees are the Fixed Signs, they codify those actions into a system. The final 30 degrees are the Mutable Signs, that apply those actions and systems in human situations.

Then the next season begins with the next Cardinal Sign. Signs of the same Quality are separated from each other by either 90 or 180 degrees. Those "Aspects", the Square and Opposition, are considered challenging, but productive relationships. So, the Cardinal Sign Aries is 90 degrees from the Cardinal Signs Cancer and Capricorn, and 180 degrees from the Cardinal Signs Libra.

How the Sequence of the Signs Works

The 12 Signs make a sequential cycle that contains the three finer cycles. First: The Signs alternate from Dynamic to Receptive, starting with Dynamic Aries and ending with Receptive Pisces. Second: They start with the Fire Sign Aries to Earth Sign Taurus to Air Sign Gemini to Water Sign Cancer, then back to Fire Sign Leo and so on. Third: They start with the Cardinal Sign Aries, followed by Fixed Taurus and Mutable Gemini, then back to Cardinal Cancer and so on. These three imbedded cycles;
Polarity, Element and Quality (or standing) tell you how the Signs act and how they relate to each other. This is important because life is all about roles and relationships!

What the Three Definitions Tell Us About the Signs

First: Signs of similar **Polarity** (Receptive or Dynamic) are mildly supportive of each other and are separated by multiples of 60 degrees. Example: The first degree of Dynamic Aries is 60 degrees from the first degree of the next Dynamic Sign Gemini. That Aspect, 60 degrees, is called a Sextile. Aries is a Fire Sign and Gemini is an Air Sign, so they are they both related to Father Sky. The next Sextile in the sequence, Receptive Earth Sign Taurus and Receptive Water Sign Cancer are both linked to Mother Earth.

Second: Signs of the same **Element** are very supportive of each other and connected by multiples of 120 degree, an Aspect called a Trine. Example: The first degree of the Air Sign Gemini is 120 degrees from the first degree of Air Signs Libra and Aquarius. In simplified Sun Sign Astrology people are often advised to find a partner in one of the other two related Element Signs.
For example, a Virgo Sun should seek a Taurus or Capricorn Sun. As we said, relationships are everything.

In Chinese Astrology people are advised to find a mate four years older or younger than themselves. That is because their Jupiter positions will be in the same element, or Trine. For example, someone born in the Year of the Rabbit (Jupiter in Aries) should marry someone born in the Year or the Sheep (Jupiter in Leo) or the Year of the Pig (Jupiter in Sagittarius), the three Western Fire Signs. This promotes fiscal stability and mutual good luck. Sound advice!

Third: Signs having a similar **Quality** or Standing challenge each other to be productive and are connected by Aspects of 90 degrees (Square) and 180 degrees (Opposition). Example: The first degree of the Fixed Sign Taurus is 90 degrees from the first degrees of Leo and Aquarius and 180 degrees from the first
degree of Scorpio.

Some Observations about the Seasons

In Western Astrology the year starts with Spring at the first degree of the Sign Aries. But, in Asia, the Springtime festival, called the Chinese New Year, begins at the New Moon in Aquarius, which can occur any time between the 19th of January and the 18th of February. That is where the concept of an early or late Spring comes from, that we celebrate on Groundhog Day. The Aquarius New Moon is when the energy of the Earth is drawn in.

In the northern hemisphere, it is after that New Moon when the seeds begin to stir in the moist, darkness of the Earth. Western Astrology, a Yang culture, prefers aggressive Aries as the starting point because that is when that new growth's red shoots burst into the light. Red is the color of the Planet Mars who rules Aries. Asia prefers Aquarius, a Sign that denies the ego in favor of the common good.

The 3 Signs of Spring: Aries, Taurus, Gemini

♈ ♉ ♊

In Western Astrology the 3 Signs of Spring are Aries, when the first buds appear, **Taurus** when the green leaves unfurl and **Gemini** when the flying insects begin buzzing about spreading the pollen. **Aries** is a Dynamic, Cardinal Fire Sign ruled by Mars and symbolized by the Ram, because it is an impetuous, lustful time of year. **Taurus** is a Receptive, Fixed Earth Sign ruled by Venus and symbolized by the Bull (although a Cow is a better description since it is a Receptive Sign) because it is patient and stable.

Gemini is a Dynamic, Mutable Air Sign ruled by Mercury and symbolized by the Twins. It is associated with the twin brothers, Romulus and Remus, who established Rome and were known for their joint talents of enterprise and mischief.

The 3 Signs of Summer: Cancer, Leo, Virgo

♋ ♌ ♍

The first day of Summer begins with Cancer, a Receptive, Cardinal Water Sign ruled by the Moon, symbolized by the Crab and associated with the sea, the tides, the Mother and the home-life. The Sign is closely associated with mothering and the first nurturing liquid the child experiences, the maternal milk. This is the season when the flowers turn into the first edible fruits.

That is followed by Leo, a Dynamic, Fixed Fire Sign ruled by the Sun and symbolized by the Lion, the King of the Jungle. Now the trees are filled with fruit for the picking and there is an abundance of flowers for both vitamins and matters of the heart. These first two Signs relate to the high Summer when the living is easy, and people go on vacation.

The third Summer Sign is Virgo, a Receptive, Mutable, Earth Sign ruled by Mercury and symbolized by the Virgin. Virgo is the largest stellar constellation and before the Christian Era these Stars were known as the 'Great Goddess'. This is harvest time and Virgo's legendary industriousness, attention to detail and cleanliness describes the diligent efforts of gathering and sorting fruit, vegetables, grains and winemaking.

History says that it was women who led humanity from the hunter gatherer life to agriculture, by cultivating storable grains and grasses at the riversides. Virgo is when the family and the community work together quickly and efficiently, to bring in the grapes for wine and the grains and beans as staples to last them through the Winter.

Because girls mature faster than boys and often have better dexterity, their contribution was especially prized at the close of Summer, when harvest requires patient, skilled hands.

The 3 Signs of Autumn: Libra, Scorpio, Sagittarius

♎ ♏ ♐

The first day of Autumn begins with Libra, a Dynamic, Cardinal Air Sign ruled by Venus and symbolized by the Scales. It is related to partnerships and marriage because this is when each family's seasonal contribution and share is carefully and fairly measured on the scales.

As the leaves disappear and the first Signs of Winter make their appearance **Scorpio begins**, a Receptive, Fixed, Water Sign ruled by Mars and symbolized by the Scorpion, although it is alternately symbolized by the Snake, the Eagle and the Phoenix.

It traditionally relates to the cooperative use of power. As the rains bring the harvest to a close and the leaves fall away serious, private tasks are required with the approaching Winter, so the bargaining gets tougher and secrets more vital. The hard frosts set in at higher elevations and the first ice, or Fixed Water, appears on the ponds.

As the last leaves are gone **Sagittarius** begins, a Dynamic, Mutable, Fire Sign ruled by giant Jupiter and symbolized by the Centaur Archer. This is the time when the views expand with the first frosts, the protective cover of leaves is gone, and the hunters venture out.

With a patron like Zeus, aka the 'Big Guy in the Plaid Suit', for his wonderfully colorful, swirling surface, it is unsurprising that 'Sag' is known for optimism, philosophy, travel and entrepreneurship.

The 3 Signs of Winter: Capricorn, Aquarius, Pisces

♑ ♒ ♓

The first day of Winter begins with Capricorn, a Receptive, Cardinal, Earth Sign ruled by Saturn and symbolized by the Sea Goat, a Goat with the tail of a Fish. Traditionally it relates to time and maturity. Where Sagittarius expands, Capricorn contracts. This is when Winter sets in seriously, everything contracts with the cold and wood is brought in to fuel the fire. It is a Sign that deals with prestige because the success of the year's efforts will show in the quality of the winter coats you and your family are wearing at the Winter Solstice Festival.

As Winter deepens, **Aquarius** begins, a Dynamic, Fixed, Air Sign also ruled by Saturn and symbolized by the Water Bearer, although some experts say it is the Water Pourer. The symbol relates to the innovation of irrigation at the beginning of the agricultural era. This is the time of year when rice farmers drain and repair their growing ponds. Aquarius is about community action for the common good, your social connections and friendships. It describes the community that your history and efforts have given you access to.

Winter ends with **Pisces**, a Receptive, Mutable, Water Sign ruled by Jupiter and symbolized by Two Fishes, one swimming towards the deep and another swimming towards the light. In Pisces Winter begins to lose its grip, the hard ground is thawing, the melting snow softens the seeds helping their germination. The hint of Spring is bringing hope as is suitable for a Sign ruled by expansive Jupiter. With the completion of Pisces, we find ourselves once again hopefully approaching the first day of Spring and the new cycle.

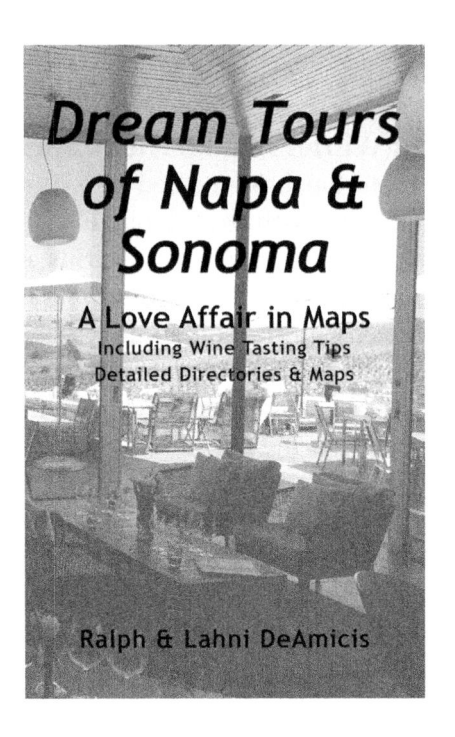

Chapter Four is an
excerpt from the book

'Dream Tours of Napa & Sonoma
A Love Affair in Maps'

This is the newest edition of our series of tour and travel books we have been producing about wine country since 2007!

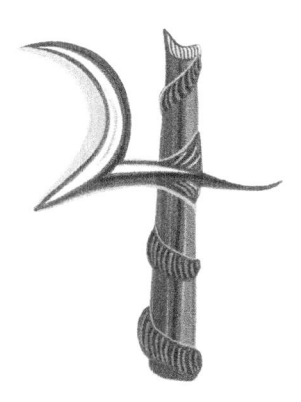

Chapter Four: Ralph's ABC's for Tasting Wine

The way you drink wine with a meal is different from how you sample it in a tasting room. The funny techniques you see people using during tastings help them perceive the wine better through the senses of sight, scent and taste. It starts with the glassware. Wineries use crystal goblets because they are rougher than glass. When you swirl the wine, those microscopic bumps pull apart its molecules, mixing them with oxygen, releasing the aromas and flavors for you to experience. Hint: The fancier the winery the fancier the glasses.

Start by holding the glass by the stem. It is partly to prevent your hand from warming the wine, but mostly because that makes it easier to move the wine around inside the glass. Temperature matters and wines are poured at different temperatures; sparkling and sweet whites are the coldest while the dry whites and light reds are cool. The big red wines start out at 'cellar' temperatures and then gradually warm during the tasting, which allows the complex flavors to bloom. The worst thing you can do is not give the wine a chance to open up and stretch, after its long seclusion in the bottle. That's like having the genie pop out of the lamp and not giving them time to properly introduce themselves before you start asking them to grant your wishes.

Start by holding the glass upright and taking a sniff. Much of what you're smelling at the top of the glass is alcohol rising off the liquid. Next, set the glass on the tabletop (the tasting notes make a nice, soft surface), place your fingers firmly on top of the base and vigorously swirl the wine clockwise. Now, pick the glass up and hold it to the light. Wine is a complex creation so you may see red, blue, violet, gold, straw and so on, depending on the varietal. Set the glass down and swirl it again.

Next, pick up the glass and hold it at a 45-degree angle across your body (so you avoid pouring the wine on yourself), and put your nose on the glass' lower lip, and take a sniff. At this angle, the alcohol fumes are rising inside the globe, and slipping out at the top like smoke going up a chimney, happily bypassing your nose. Now, instead of mostly smelling alcohol, you're smelling the heavier fruit flavors below, the wonderful scent of fermented grapes!

Take a moment to appreciate the bouquet. With a big, densely flavored red wine, it's best to repeat the swirl and sniff steps a few times, until you've truly captured the fullness of the scent, before taking a sip. With a white wine the flavors open more quickly and you can move through swirl, sniff and sip in three lovely steps. Then just keep repeating the process until there is none left.

Wine Geek Alert! There is an odd phenomenon that happens with wines that have been aged in oak for an extended period, usually eighteen months or more. As related to me by winemakers, when you swirl the wine clockwise you will smell predominantly fruit flavors. But when you swirl counterclockwise, you will also notice the nutty, sometimes spicy flavors that come from the barrel. Why does this happen? According to Ralph's best quasi-scientific analysis, it is due to the relative efficiency of vortices. A clockwise swirl more efficiently mixes the various part of the wine together. But the less efficient counterclockwise swirl allows the layers to separate. The wooden barrel flavors are the last ones to be infused into the juice and in this less organized mix, some of those woody notes are left floating at the top for your nose to discover. This technique is used by some winemakers to determine a barrel's influence on the wine. If you have a good sense of smell, you will notice the difference. Now you are officially a Wine Geek!

When you take a sip, move the wine around your mouth, so it touches all your taste buds from the tip of your tongue to the valley in its center, and then, both sides. Once the flavors are well dispersed, you can swallow the sip. There are certain scent notes that are only released when they touch your tongue. To access them, gently breathe in through your mouth so the aromas on your palate reach your nose via the back of your throat. There is another quality you should note called 'mouth feel'. It is how the texture of the wine feels to the surface of your mouth. Is it sharply acidic, soothingly silky, or almost sticky and syrupy?

That gives you some clues about the kinds of foods and situations the wine is suited for. A high acid wine goes great with food because it cleans the palate and helps the digestion. A wine with a soft mouth feel is nice at a party for socializing. The syrupy sweet wines make a nice dessert after a heavy meal, when you don't have room for cake.

One 'mouth feel' to watch out for is the almost flame-like touch of a high alcohol, dry wine, which is why that kind of wine is called 'hot'. Port is also high in alcohol, but the wine is heavy and sweet, so the alcohol is deeply embedded in the flavors. But, many of the most expensive Cabernet blends are quite hot, at 15% to 16% alcohol, while totally dry (meaning that all the grape sugar has been converted to alcohol). If the dehydrating alcohol is not well moderated and integrated into the wine, it will feel like a sip dries out your tongue and you may be thirstier after the tasting than before you began.

With these steps, you have experienced almost the full signature of the wine; the look, scent, flavor and feel. The only note still missing is how the alcohol hits you. Popular wines range from about 10% up to 16% alcohol. Port is fortified with grape spirits to stop the fermentation before the sugar is completely consumed, and it is about 20% alcohol. A wine below 12% is called a table wine, and for many years most wines were in that range. The change happened due to the desire for bigger, fuller flavored wines, which requires leaving the grapes on the vines longer, where they make more sugar, which the yeast converts into more alcohol.

Related to inebriation, not every wine makes you feel the same. We suppose this is because wines are chemically complex nutrition and your body uses the dietary components it encounters. The best wines are also the healthiest, because they are pure, they contain a higher quality alcohol and more vital nutrients, so your body recognizes it as 'good' food. Eating more vital foods helps you feel optimistic, confident, content and loved. This is not scientifically quantifiable, but it is clear from experience that some wines make you feel 'better' than others.

The Importance of Swirling

We cannot repeat this enough, swirling is essential. A great deal of effort and technology goes into keeping the wine away from any oxygen that will dissipate its flavors. Mixing the wine with air inside the glass releases those trapped aromas and flavors, making them available to your nose and tongue. Swirling the glass by sitting its base on a tabletop produces much better aeration than swirling it while you hold up in your hand. It also keeps the wine stains off your clothes, which happen most often later in the day when you loosen up. Even the best wineries don't have carpets in their tasting rooms for a reason.

The nose detects millions of scents, many more than we can identify. But the palate is more limited. Conventional wisdom says there are only six or seven main flavors that people can describe. You have probably heard the list; sweet, sour, salty, bitter, pungent and astringent with 'umami' being a recent addition. We detect more nuances, but flavors defy verbal description because they are experienced in the body's language center and they take up the full band width. That's why great flavors can render you speechless. It's hard to describe a taste in detail because 'flavor' is its own language.

The First Sip Conundrum

While all these techniques sound thoroughly enjoyable, there is a hurdle to overcome. That first sip of the day rarely tastes good. Why? Because much of what you will be initally tasting is your breakfast, or maybe your toothpaste, still stuck on your tongue! The same thing happens after lunch, but to a lesser extent. The wineries know about this, so that is why they start with a high acid, white wine, to clean your palate and warm up your taste buds. Once your palate is clean and tuned it's clear sailing.

It is important to give your nose and palate time to wake up and adapt to the situation so do not rush the first tasting. In your everyday life those two sensory organs experience the same group of scents and flavors in the same sequence with little variation. They are nice aromas, familiar flavors, comforting to your emotions and sometimes delivering valuable messages, like that afternoon cup of coffee when you need to get back to work. At a wine tasting you are asking your palate to analyze a series of complex wines containing hundreds of scents and flavors, one after another. So start off slowly and don't worry, it's like playing a sport, after a little warm up, you will find that everything moves. feels and even tastes right.

A Tour Guide's Napa Valley

The Secrets for Enjoying the World Famous Wineries
Including Wine Tasting Tips
Maps & a Detailed Directory

Ralph & Lahni De Amicis

Chapter Five is an excerpt from

'A Tour Guide's Napa Valley, The Secrets for Enjoying the World Famous Wineries'

There is a twin book called 'A Tour Guide's Sonoma Wine Country'

Chapter Five: Our Best Tasting Room Tips

What will the tasting room host expect from you? They'll expect you to enjoy! They do not expect you to be a wine expert, that's their job. As a wine tourist, what are you an expert about? The wines you like! That's because you have a library of scents and flavors from every wine you have ever tasted. The limbic part of your brain, where scent, flavor and emotion live, never forgets those experiences, including where you were and how you felt. Your wine preferences are uniquely yours, based on that amazing mix of deep memories, adjusted for your evolving physiology. That's because the sensitivity of your senses changes over time as your nutritional demands shift.

One of the first questions we ask new clients is their age because of the evolution of the palate. We suggest places that make wines that are appealing to their generation, but with some exceptions. For example, while younger people generally like light bodied wines like Chardonnay, Pinot Grigio and Pinot Noir, those working in high finance often go for the expensive Cabernets. Those are normally an older man's wine; full flavored, tannin rich and suited to a less sensitive palate that craves sulfur. Another example: we normally expect the Boomers to like those Cabs, but if they are fitness enthusiasts, their healthier, hyper-sensitive palates often prefer white and sparkling wines.

There are good reasons why the most often heard phrase in tasting rooms is, "The best wines are the ones you like".

They typically pour four to five wines, starting with a high acid white to clean the palate, followed by increasingly bigger and darker wines, saving the most expensive for the end. Each sample is supposedly one ounce. If they are using the same glass for the entire tasting don't worry about the flavors mixing, since each stronger flavor overwrites the previous. Don't rinse the glass with water between wines because the water coating will interfere with your tongue's sensitivity.

Sometimes the lineup of wines are arranged side by side in multiple glasses. This gives them time to open up properly and it lets you revisit them. Vertical tastings of the same wine from different vintages were once more popular. This is a European tradition for wineries that make one wine, where different years produce varied results. But North Bay wineries, thanks to the remarkable climate, have a wide variety of high-quality wines to show off, and visitors who are adventurous in their tastes.

Bigger wineries have wider selections of wines, both standard and reserve lists, plus food pairings. Smaller wineries have one list. Don't assume the reserve wines will taste better. They are chosen because they age well, and their current flavors may be less appealing.

Not all tasting room staff are equally knowledgeable. In the slow season, the managers and professionals are pouring, but in the Summer, less experienced, part-timers often work in the tasting rooms. Ask your concierge or tour guide to recommend a particular host who is known for their knowledge and fun style.

The amount of time they spend with you depends on how busy they are. Year round on the weekends, large wineries can be slammed but even in the high season, especially during the week, there are plenty of small wineries looking for guests. If you want to learn more about wine, do the seated tasting, because hosts often only work with one group at a time, so you get more personalized attention.

The typical lineup starts with a white wine such as the popular Chardonnay, especially in cooler Sonoma. It is a muscular grape that handles higher alcohol levels, that can be made crisp in stainless steel tanks, or barrel aged for a toasted, buttery caramel flavored wine, with hints of chocolate and nuts. Those buttery Chardonnays were a gateway wine for many beer and spirit drinkers because that collection of flavors is remarkably similar to Coca Cola.

In Napa, a popular first wine may be Sauvignon Blanc which grows beside the Cabernet and Merlot. Locals like it because it ripens earlier, so it doesn't compete for production tank space and it's ready to sell the following Spring, while the other wines are still aging in their barrels. Fermented in stainless steel, it makes a crisp, refreshing low alcohol wine that goes great with lighter fare.

When it is aged in new, toasted oak barrels it produces the smoky Fume' style. While most people drink it young, laying a good one down for a decade produces wonderful depth and smoothness with a honeyed nose. Harvested late, after it has been desiccated by the botrytis fungus, it becomes the costly, golden sweet Sauternes. Other possibilities for a first wine, depending on location and the winemaker's need for a diversion, are Pinot Grigio, Riesling, Chenin Blanc, or a signature blend. Tasting Hint: It is important to manage your alcohol intake. If you are not a fan of white wines, ask your host to skip them. Next come the red wines, from lightest to heaviest. In cooler areas like southern Napa, and southern and coastal Sonoma, that's Pinot Noir and Syrah.

In the warmer sections of Sonoma, Petite Syrah and Zinfandel are popular. In the warmest areas (Napa Valley and Alexander Valley) the grapes of Bordeaux rule: Cabernet Sauvignon, Merlot, Cabernet Franc, Malbec and Petite Verdot. Here and there you will find a few pockets of Italy's Sangiovese and Barbera, and Spain's Tempranillo. But please realize that we are dramatically understating the possibilities of what you might taste, because over a hundred different grape varietals thrive in the diverse and hospitable North Bay climate.

There are numerous heritage vineyards planted by the orginal immigrant generations containing obscure varietals. Just over the eastern hills from Napa, Portuguese families planted their own varietals that thrive in the windy Suisun Valley. This wide variety, coupled with excellent quality, makes the North Bay Wine Country a popular destination for the grape varietal adventurer, and yes, that's a thing!

About the Authors

Ralph and Lahni DeAmicis got into writing tour books through a project about the Napa and Sonoma wineries. It was supposed to be the fourth book in their Feng Shui series. They had been speaking on Feng Shui for many years and are the current authors of the Planetary Calendar, America's preeminent astrology calendar started in 1949.

To help the research along Ralph got a part-time job driving wine tours. They quickly realized that even though the wineries are the region's main attraction, there weren't any 'winery' tour books. The big, widely distributed wineries got most of the business, while the small, family wineries struggled to attract customers. Ralph and Lahni loved visiting the family wineries, so their project morphed into their first guidebook in 2008. Eight editions later they are the region's most popular winery tour books, and a valued resource for the guides and concierges. Meanwhile the Planetary Calendar is going strong in its 75th year.

Ralph & Lahni started Amicis Tours in 2007, which makes their ongoing research easier. Through observing thousands of wine tastings, Ralph saw how much both the surroundings and the Moon Sign affected the guest's experience of the wine. They realized that the 'good or bad' definitions for the Moon positions offered by BioDynamics were too simple, and sometimes simply wrong. They saw for themselves that every day is good for wine tasting, but what changes is the type of experience the participants enjoy the most.

So, they documented what they saw, paired it with chapters from three other books and created their first wine tasting calendar in 2023. Today, Ralph and Lahni are popular guides who work in multiple languages, and who speak to groups about the Wine Country Experience, Feng Shui, Astrology and, of course Wine Tasting with the Stars.

Find their Wine Country books on Amazon
Find more at www.Planetary Calendar.com

Cuore Libre Publishing
Books and Calendars

A Tour Guide's Napa Valley
A Tour Guide's Sonoma Wine Country
Dream Tours of Napa & Sonoma
Wine Country in Shorts, Stories of Napa and Sonoma
The Sonoma Navigator, The Napa Navigator
Watch the Author's TV Show 'Wine Country in Shorts'

PlanetaryCalendar.com

Published Annually since 1949
Planetary Calendar Astrology with Forecasts
Two Wall Sizes, a Pocket Size, a Day Planner,
Digital Version & Companion Book
'PCA: Moving Beyond Observation to Action'
The Lunar Wine Tasting Calendar
Watch Monthy Video Forecasts
@PlanetaryCalendarAstrology on YouTube.

Ralph & Lahni De Amicis are authors, storytellers, astrologers, and video producers in Napa California. They consult with clients, do speeches, lead workshops and conduct private tours throughout the North Bay Wine Country. This Calendar started as the seminar materials for their workshop, Wine Tasting with the Stars. It mixes two of their favorite topics, Astrology and Wine Country.

You can contact them at www.PlanetaryCalendar.com.

Printed in Great Britain
by Amazon